City Comforts

HOW TO BUILD AN URBAN VILLAGE

City Comforts

HOW TO BUILD AN URBAN VILLAGE

DAVID SUCHER

City Comforts Inc.

SEATTLE | 2003

First Edition Thank-Yous

Many people made valuable suggestions about early drafts or simply helped by their conversation, and I would like to thank them: Brian Dudgeon, Clair Enlow, Rich Untermann, Tony Puma, Gerry Johnson, Laurie Sucher, Julia Walton, David Wright, Donald K. Erickson, Marcia Wagoner, Michael Reed, Scott Flett. Some people read drafts with particularly active red pencils, and I thank them, too: Fire Cruxent, Donald Padelford, Penelope Bell, and John Davies.

In particular I would like to recognize Magrit Baurecht for graphic design, Alexander Zatko of Pine Tree Design for pre-press, Marilyn Meyer for editing and a parent's-eye view, and Barbara Gray for research assistance. I would like to especially thank Christopher K. Leman for his editing ideas and his very helpful conversation about transportation.

Many thanks to my special friend Elizabeth Kanny, without whose down-to-earth common sense this book would be titled something like *An Empirical Approach to Optimum Urban Development with Reference to Specific Elements of the Physical Infrastructure Conducive to Increased Social Interaction* and you would not be reading even this far.

Thanks also to a friend who pointed out — as I procrastinated about releasing the manuscript to the printer — that architects have an apt saying: "Better built than perfect."

Second Edition Thank-Yous

My much-belated thanks to Mark Hinshaw, who first introduced me to the notion that there is an elegant simplicity and only a very few elements to making a great street.

My much-belated thanks as well to Witold Rybcyznski, who in his book *Home* put me on the path of comfort in cities. He wrote, "During the six years of my architectural education, the subject of comforts was mentioned only once . . . . It was a curious omission in an otherwise rigorous criticism; one would have thought that comfort was a crucial issue in preparing for the architectural profession, like justice in law, or health in medicine." So too, I thought, for city planning.

Thanks also to Barbara Sjoholm, Marilyn Meyer (editing), and Miriam Bulmer (editing and proofreading), Magrit Baurecht (graphic design), Tim Crosby (photo imaging), Barbara Gray (technical consulting and indexing), and Carl Juarez (final layout, design and image assistance).

Thanks as well to critical readers Elizabeth Kanny, Michelle Coad, and Mary Alice.

Copyright © 2003 by David Sucher
ISBN 0-9642680-1-9
Library of Congress Control Number: 2002093124
Second printing 2007

Photographs by David Sucher except as noted
Illustrations by Kevin Kane

CONTENTS

CHAPTER 1

Anywhere, U.S.A.

HOW TO BUILD AN URBAN VILLAGE
Dystopia

The picture above shows the kind of spread-out, auto-dominated world that we are trying to avoid. If you do not agree, read no further. This book is not an attempt to persuade you that a compact, walkable city is good for you or better for your health, like a diet, though that may well be so. The author assumes that the reader already prefers "real" cities and neighborhoods, of Jane Jacobs–type diversity and grain; the only question is how to foster them.

City Comforts outlines the simple rules and details that create pedestrian-oriented, comfortable neighborhoods and cities. It rejects ambitious mega-projects as nonessential or even undesirable.

I begin with the "Three Rules of Urban Design." I'll explain more later, but here are the essentials:

1. Build to the sidewalk (i.e., property line).

2. Make the building front "permeable" (i.e., no blank walls).

3. Prohibit parking in front of the building.

These rules are the starting point for zoning and designing walkable streets.

Then I show the host of simple details (characterized as "city comforts") that make a place human. The details I offer are merely the tip of the iceberg. Human adaptation to the environment is extremely rich. This book is by no means exhaustive but merely, and even meagerly, illustrative.

HOW THIS BOOK CAME TO BE

The work of Christopher Alexander was inspirational. In an essay, "Cities as a Mechanism for Sustaining Human Contact," he says that people come together in cities not only for the traditional reasons of trade, politics, and security, but because cities allow people the chance to increase their human closeness. The way to measure the success of a city, he says, is by how well it fosters and encourages human communication.

It is often said that cities are like giant telephone switching systems whose function is to put people into contact. But this is an imperfect analogy; with the telephone system one knows who one is calling. The wonderful thing about cities is that they can connect people who did not know each other before.

Then, and more strikingly, I found Alexander's small but rich book, *A Pattern Language*. This book is an important one. Alexander and his team examined the built environment and extracted from it what they thought were a set of rules — the patterns — for good building and comfortable living.

One need not agree with all the particular patterns shown in *A Pattern Language* — I find it a bit doctrinaire about mass society. But the book was groundbreaking for me because it pointed out that there are widely held patterns of subjective reaction to the built environment. There exist archetypes of designs that work, have worked for thousands of years, and will likely work far into the future.

Contrary to what is often said, the built environment is not all a matter of taste. Some solutions to a design problem work better than others. Each pattern is a way to solve an environmental problem in making the world comfortable. There is, in fact, a great deal of social agreement about what works and what doesn't in the built environment. The disagreements are largely at the margins.

I once served on a citizens' advisory committee. The city was developing policies to regulate building size, shape, and so on. Our group of citizens met many times, and I gradually noticed a pattern in our conversations. We never talked about specifics but only about diffuse abstractions. It was as if we were afraid to grapple with concrete reality. Or perhaps we lacked the vocabulary to speak intelligibly about the built environment. There was something enormously dead about our conversation.

I thought of D. H. Lawrence's gamekeeper who said that he "canna love a woman who canna piss or shit." We never spoke of specific buildings or specific landscapes that were thought either horrendous or worthy of emulation.

The neighbor types spoke — on and on and on — of "excessive height, bulk, and scale" and, on the other side, the developers orated about "affordable housing." But there was no talk of real buildings or landscapes, no informal discussion about this or that project, no complaint about this or praise of that. No shop talk about architecture or design.

I grew confused. I wanted to hear specifics. Where were buildings? Where was landscape? Where was the ostensible subject at hand? Was it truly land and buildings? Or, indeed, was the subject simply power? Our discussions were not about the real material city of buildings and streets. We were supposed to advise a government about how it should regulate the way people shape their buildings, yet our conversations never moved beyond code words.

The solution, I realized, was to focus on specific details of the built environment. Let's reverse-engineer — let's work backwards, empirically, from *post hoc* rather than *a priori*. Let's examine our city; let's pick out those things that please us and then design our land-use codes around those pleasing models. Let's do what all practical people do: copy what works and not reinvent the wheel with each new building. Only to someone who has never worked with local zoning boards would such an approach appear obvious.

So why *City Comforts*?

It struck me as useful that we should talk to each other — when we talk about the built environment at all — by referring to specific details of the city. Builders, neighbors, administrators, politicians, even designers, might find it useful to have a book filled with pictures of specific ways that have already been used in real situations to deal with real and very specific problems. We reason by analogy — would not pictures aid the process?

Our land-use codes are phrased more to prevent bad things than to encourage the good. Think of the law as an ongoing conversation in which the majority is speaking about what is appropriate to build. People in real conversations constantly use examples to better communicate their desires. Why not the land-use laws as well? They are a conversation between society and individual about how and what to build. So let the conversation proceed with reference to real examples.

My own research methodology

It may be sadly obvious that this book started with no outline. I simply started taking pictures of things that seemed significant and that seemed to "work." In many cases I wasn't sure at first what exactly was working.

Some pictures still lie on my desk. I believe they work and are important in some way — at least they caught my eye — but I haven't figured them out yet. There is great significance in even the most mundane things around us, if we but look at them.

WHAT TO EXPECT OF THIS BOOK

City Comforts is not about any particular city. A large number of the photographs were taken in and near Seattle, Washington. But that's only because I live here. The photos simply show, by and large, *types*. In fact, better examples might very well exist in other cities (and I would appreciate knowing of them).

City Comforts presents a metaphor — the urban village — as a way of describing the mix of intimacy and anonymity that I believe most people desire and that is largely missing in our large urban settlements.

Too much discussion is devoted to grand strategic visions. Certainly those are important. Whether or not we build more mass transit systems or where we place a major public facility such as an airport are certainly decisions with long legs. Many, if not most, regions are groping toward an urban containment policy to hold back urban sprawl and create denser cities through reweaving the tears in the urban fabric.

But no matter what the investment or the strategy, what is important for the individual human being is how the city works at the personal level. Small details at the individual level are where a municipal strategy fails or succeeds. For want of a nail, the kingdom was lost.

This book is an attempt to refocus our public policy discussion from abstract generalities, colored maps, and grandiose projects to the details that create our daily experience. It demonstrates a way of looking at and speaking about our immediate environment.

Talk precedes action

This book emphasizes the importance of public and private conversation in creating the reality we have around us. In Homer's epics the characters speak and describe what they will do before they do it. To take poetic license with Churchill, "We build our cities first with words and then with bricks."

Many of these small details are so obvious as to be invisible

This book shows examples of small things — city comforts — that make urban life pleasant: places where people can meet; methods to tame cars and to make buildings good neighbors; art that infuses personality into locations and makes them into places. It is not even remotely an attempt to cover the field completely. The diversity and imagination of human beings in creating their settlements are far too vast for one book.

The keys to transforming our cities into places of comfort and delight are in plain view and not in the least bit concealed or mysterious or accessible only to obscure expertise. Like Poe's purloined letter, they are so plainly visible that our eyes skip over them. We do not imagine that the ordinary is worthy of serious consideration, so it escapes attention, much less serious discussion.

WHAT THIS BOOK IS NOT ABOUT

Not about design as expensive

City comfort is not about good design as a status symbol, as a slightly subtle way to indicate wealth; it's not about fancy and it's not about fashion. Good design is not about spending a lot of money and hiring big-name architects, though money doesn't hurt and famous architects may well be first-rate and deserve their fame. Good design is thoughtful and well mannered. It's not about pretty but about comfort. Of course, if it is pretty it may also become more comfortable — but aesthetics alone do not make for comfort. It's not about visual statements and grand intellectual constructs. Good design is about creating certain feelings of ease and restfulness. City comfort is design as forethought and consideration for the user.

Not about density as a goal for its own sake

Urban planners are often not aware of the market; the surest sign is that very early in any discussion of urban form they will start talking about density and units per acre. But these terms are hard to visualize for citizens who must understand these plans if they are to succeed. I have been working around land and buildings for thirty years, and when a planner talks about increasing the density of an area from six to forty units per acre I have no idea what is meant without painfully translating those numbers into a specific picture. It is the feel of a neighborhood that is important to people, not its numerical density.

Moreover, in the abstract, density is a scare word and hardly persuasive. Certainly, the interesting parts of town are dense. No question. But the density is simply a by-product of people trying to be at the same interesting spot. One doesn't start with density. Certainly one doesn't start the political process with density. One ends with density because a place is diverse and intriguing and people want to be there.

Rather than argue for concentration of people, we identify the small things — city comforts — that draw people together into denser settlements and make the mixing and mingling a pleasure rather than a dose of cod liver oil.

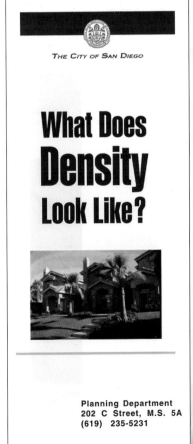

THE CITY OF SAN DIEGO

What Does Density Look Like?

Planning Department
202 C Street, M.S. 5A
(619) 235-5231

Not about rail transit per se

As pointed out in Chapter 4, "Getting Around," any discussion of urban villages is sure to include pleas for mass transit. Getting people out of their cars has become a gospel. But this book is not about prayers and wishful thinking.

Debates about mass transit elicit statements of fervent faith and devolve into technical debates. But I am agnostic. Mass transit may have a significant effect; it depends on how it is done. It is not a panacea. As Walter Pater said, "Style is everything." Rail (heavy, light, mono-) or road, cities based on either technology can be better designed than they are now, and neither is the key to creating comfortable communities.

A further danger is that debates on rail — to build or not — will consume enormous energy and become an issue in themselves: an example of the end being consumed by the process. And then, if an action is approved by the political process, we will think that the problem is solved and continue to build uncomfortable cities because we focus on the forest and ignore the trees.

Furthermore, many of us live in settlements where population density is so low that rail will not be feasible—even in the eyes of enthusiastic advocates—for decades, at best. If we depend on a massive investment in heavy fixed-rail systems, as some propose, to create comfortable cities and urban villages, we may be very disappointed. We had better figure out how to make those vast suburbs, too, more civil now, and without the remotest expectation of rail.

To paraphrase an expression from *Alice in Wonderland,* when the Queen described jam as something for yesterday and tomorrow but no other day, rail transit is jam yesterday, jam tomorrow, but never jam today. Rail transit is an example of the "I'll be happy when . . ." phenomenon, but on a societal level. It's a way of avoiding dealing with problems now and hoping that one big thing —in the future — will solve them.

So I urge caution. Build multibillion-dollar heavy rail systems if you like. But expect no magical creation of comfortable cities.

Not about government projects

Interesting neighborhoods evolve one building at a time, and largely by individuals. Of course the government must set a level playing field of sensible ground rules. But the basic rules needed to create the physical context for comfortable settlements are not complicated. The politics and education needed to let people see the basic simplicity of these rules may be difficult — Poe's purloined letter shows that the obvious is sometimes invisible.

The creation of community — fundamentally based on the relations between people — is largely beyond the reach of government, and the sooner we understand that the better. Otherwise we'll wait a long time for government (or any other large organization, for that matter) to build urban villages, and then they may be named Potemkin.

HOW TO USE THIS BOOK

This book offers workable responses to typical problems of the urban landscape. It's obviously neither a textbook nor an encyclopedia. It's a personal statement of what I have observed and believe to be important. It's not meant to be a complete or systematic study.

So, other than the simply curious, there are four groups of people who may benefit from this book: neighbors, architects, municipal officials, and property owners.

Neighbors could use this book to talk with developers and tinker with projects. More often than not, neighbors are at a loss to deal with developers effectively. They often approach new development with the not-in-my-backyard attitude. Though they may claim the high moral ground of speaking for "the community," little conversation is needed to see that some, at least, are out to protect their own vested interests — the on-street parking space in front of their own house, for example.

Neighbors too often start from a viewpoint — more accurate as an exception than as the rule — that development can actually be stopped. Our system of local government taxation and administration is biased in favor of development. Fairly often, neighbors attempt to stop a project and end up with high legal bills and a project exactly or virtually the same as first proposed.

More productive would be an approach that — grudgingly but realistically — accepts impending change but attempts to mold it into a more civil and comfortable form. It would be more productive for neighbors to go to a developer and say something like "Look. We're not really happy about any change in our neighborhood and we're not sure how far we will go in contesting you. But perhaps, if you would change this aspect of the building here and that aspect there, we might see it differently."

Many an otherwise awful building would be quite acceptable if the developer had been encouraged to attend to the details and been aided with examples.

Architects can use this book in talking to clients and showing them possibilities that work and that may increase the attractiveness and profitability of their project, as well as speeding the permitting process, which is another form of coin.

Municipal officials, too, might use the book to communicate with proponents and opponents to show how a project might work better. People learn best and quickest when shown examples of things that have already worked for others.

The Three Rules, in particular (see page 7), go to the core of creating pedestrian-oriented places. They therefore go to the heart of simplifying land-use codes to create such neighborhoods.

Property owners can find that the creation of comfortable environments can be a rewarding endeavor, both financially and psychically. It is private initiative that will create the environments of the future. Thus, most of our effort should focus on the outlook of the property developer. Guidance from governmental authority may be necessary, but unless we want to live in a police state, we must recognize that government cannot be everywhere, and that we must rely on the property owners' own inclinations. That is not to say that the property owners are not to be bounded, but the boundaries should be based on cultural expectations, not only government rules.

The very best (and original) argument for zoning and land-use regulations is the preservation and enhancement of value, and it is that kind of argument that property owners will listen to. The designs shown in this book will increase the value of property by making it more attractive.

My goal

The author hopes that this book changes your way of looking at the city, or, at the very least, provides a few hours' diversion and amusement.

HOW TO BUILD AN URBAN VILLAGE
How seriously should we take the term "urban village"?

You'd think that just as I'm about to launch into a book of several hundred pages, I would urge splendid obeisance. Not so.

The very first mistake in creating comfortable cities would be to take the phrase too seriously. The term "urban village" is at heart a fragment of poetry. It's a metaphor and a matter of tone. It's a shorthand way of describing the feel we want from our cities. Certainly there are places that feel like an urban village, and we can use them as benchmarks. But — belying the very subtitle of this book — we can't build urban villages in one fell swoop; we watch them evolve out of a multitude of individual actions over a long period of time.

The brilliance of the phrase is that it sums up our coexisting desires for autonomy and community. We want the quiet, tree-lined street with quick access to the global market. We desire a place of repose as well as a place of activity. This tension in human relations with the environment is an old one. The phrase "urban village" is simply a way of summing it up.

Its importance is as inspiration. Musicians use a little device called a pitch pipe to help set the key when tuning an instrument. Consider the term "urban village" as a place to begin tuning our communities so that they have a certain feel.

It would be hubris to think that one can take a map of a city, start to draw lines, and say, "Inside that line is an urban village."

For one thing, it's likely to scare the citizenry. "Another new government program. Bah!" Indeed, planning bureaucracies might easily sap the vitality from the idea by overregulation, for, as we shall see, the urban village is built on only a very few but key rules.

Interesting places grow and evolve out of the intelligence of thousands of people over many years. Little could be more destructive of the urban village vision than to think of it as a particular temporal event, with a sharp boundary and a sign that announces, *Here is Urban Village No. 374. Built in 2001 by . . .*

What's important is to administer the few key rules and regulations of a city in the urban village spirit: slowly, carefully, and over a long period of time. And with a sense of humor.

A mayor's phrase

A few years ago, the then mayor of Seattle — Norman B. Rice — was speaking to the City Council about planning. In an offhand and casual way, he suggested that henceforth the city's planning would aim to build urban villages. It was genuinely a throwaway line and buried deep in his talk. But the response was galvanic. The phrase captivated people. It was seized upon. It struck a chord. It brought attention well beyond original expectation.

The urban village phrase called forth an article in *The New York Times*, where Seattle planning is hardly local news. The mayor, a good listener, made the phrase a central part of his administration's planning efforts.

At the time, I was a member of Seattle's Planning Commission. Our reaction was: "Urban village. Hmmm. What a great idea. It's brilliant. We like it. We're all in favor." Then we turned to each other and scratched our heads and asked, "What's an urban village?"

An oxymoron

At first glance the term might seem to be nonsensical and impossible: an oxymoron, the two words contradicting each other. How can you have a place that feels like a village and like a big city at the same time? The village is small, intimate, quiet; one knows the other villagers and may even be related to them. The city is big, busy, diverse, and filled with strangers. Life can be lonely in the big city. So what was the mayor talking about? What is this urban village?

The phrase "urban village" was not a new one. Sociologist Herbert Gans had spoken of "urban villagers" in the book by the same name when he studied the lives of first-generation Italian immigrants in Boston. Though these people lived in a great and urbane metropolis, their lives were bounded and limited as if they still lived in their native peasant villages. But in Seattle, the urban villagers would wear penny loafers, not peasant boots.

A phrase of contradiction

It is the contradiction that makes the phrase interesting. "Urban village" conjures two different forms of settlement (and their associated emotions) and brings them cheek by jowl. As political rhetoric, it calls for the creation of a city of contrary sensations. It is a metaphor of unusual power.

Urban	Village
hustle-bustle	tranquillity
liberty	structure
lonely	together
hostile	friendly
far away	close by
strangers	kindred
possibilities	limits

Urban	Village
growth	stasis
artificial	natural
complex	simple
large	small
skyscraper	cottage
liberal	conservative
anonymous	familiar

These words are filled with opposing emotions. The phrase drew attention and praise because people want to feel both sensations. We want to live in a city that is intimate enough so that our face is well known and respected by our local police officer. But we also want to have the privacy to make friends with people of whom our parents might not approve. We want familiarity and anonymity.

People want both

Both scales of settlement have flaws. People want the best of both worlds: the diversity, choice, and independence of the urb and the homeyness and intimacy of the village.

The political and practical challenge is to translate these two feelings — urban and village — into real streets and real buildings.

But before you can build an urban village, you have to know what it is and how to recognize one.

How to recognize an urban village

Here is one urban village indicator: while you are driving around a modern American city, you come across a commercial district where you want to get out of your car and stroll around. You have found an urban village . . . or at least a potential one.

Putting it another way, if you pass right by a parking lot and retail strip center without the slightest inclination to stop, because it does not appear interesting, you have not passed an urban village.

Although this book shows buildings and streets and related hardware, the real focus is not on physical objects but on human relations. The effort to create an urban village in physical form is only a means to an end. The means are buildings and roads and parks. The end is improved relations between people.

To a large degree, the future urban villages will emerge out of our existing neighborhoods. So it's of critical importance that we identify those things about our neighborhoods that we value and want to preserve.

Let's look at that issue a little more.

Seattle, WA

What's a neighborhood?

For a starter, what's a neighborhood? Obviously, it's a collection of physical objects: houses and streets, parks and stores. But the real importance of a neighborhood, at least to me, is that it is composed of neighbors. Neighborhoods are nothing without neighbors. It's not the buildings per se that make a neighborhood. It's the neighbors. It's the neighborliness.

And who are neighbors?

Neighbors are not simply people who live in physical proximity. Neighbors are people who are acquainted with each other, at least by sight. Neighbors have some sense of human connection. Neighbors recognize and acknowledge each other, if only with a nod of the head. Neighbors have some sense of responsibility to each other. Neighbors are not anonymous. Neighbors may have a drink together, or a potluck, or feed each other's cats when they go on vacation.

Consider some words on the neck label of Bert Grant's Celtic Ale — words written to be read and contemplated slowly, bottle in hand — and, by the way, a very nice ale:

Great ale makes great times. Great times make great friends. Great friends make great neighborhoods. Great neighborhoods make great cities. Great cities make great nations. Great nations make a great world. Therefore, the greatness of the world depends on ale. And Celtic Ale is one of the world's great ales. And only I make it. — Bert Grant

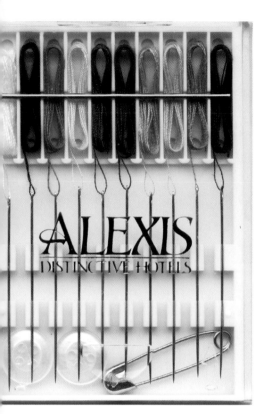

SOME OVERRIDING PRINCIPLES
Above all, attend to details

Details count. The comfortable city and the urban village are both built and experienced as a series of details, which may appear seamless and coherent, if things work well, but in fact were created over a lengthy period of time and by a variety of minds. Although a building may be very large, we perceive it detail by detail. An ordinary, even banal, structure can, and will, be transformed into a marvel if the designer and builder have thought through the users' needs and reflect those needs in details.

The sewing kit pictured here, from a hotel in Portland, Oregon, is a striking example of forethought and consideration. The harried traveler who has lost a button is saved the further vexation of threading the needle (the eye of which seems to become smaller and smaller with each passing year) by this sewing kit with pre-threaded needles.

This humble sewing kit, like the man cleaning the street of discarded bubble gum or the man showing off his sidewalk sweeper (facing page), embodies a respect for details. It is an approach to doing things that can be applied to automobiles, VCRs, and the built environment. It is a mind-set, an approach to reality that is crucial if we are to build comfortable cities. It is a mind-set that is devoted to quality, to refinement, to paying attention to details. It is a mind-set missing to some

Seattle, WA

strong degree in most of our country. We are struggling to produce excellent products for the global economy for some of the same reasons that we are struggling to create comfortable cities: we pay insufficient attention to the details.

Novelist Michael Crichton explains this approach in his novel *Rising Sun*. Two Americans are examining a new VCR made in Japan:

". . . Very neat. So small." He turned to me, holding up the box. "You know how the Japanese can make things this way and we can't? They kaizen 'em. A process of deliberate, patient, continual

Queenstown, New Zealand

refinement. Each year the products get a little better, a little cheaper. Americans don't think that way. Americans are always looking for the quantum leap, the big advance forward. Americans try to hit a home run — to knock it out of the park — and then sit back. The Japanese hit singles all day long, and they never sit back. So with something like this, you're looking at an expression of philosophy as much as anything."

Or, in other words, and paraphrasing the architect Mies van der Rohe: *God and comfort are in the details.*

Monkey see, monkey do: copy the successful

The urban design principles and details shown in this book are not new. Most have been around for hundreds or even thousands of years, and they were often better understood then.

Don't bother with originality. If you've got enormous talent, it will show; otherwise the quest for the novel for its own sake can be merely a form of self-advertising.

We are all copycats at heart. It's the way we learn as children and the way we still learn as adults. Except as adults we approach learning a little more systematically (at times) and call it reverse engineering. Most of our business culture operates in such a copycat manner: observe who is doing well, analyze the why and how, and then, to the degree allowed by the law (and sometimes beyond), do something the same way.

Our culture of building — particularly the regulatory process — could and should operate more as reverse engineering than it does. As urban planners we must consciously identify what is desirable in a particular built environment, deduce the specific rules that make these places desirable, and write the land-use codes to favor such patterns.

Sidney, BC, Canada

City comforts are in public

City comforts are small pieces of the urban landscape. To a very large degree, they involve the way the building meets the street, or the street itself, or things that can be seen from the street. Even such trivia as the shelter over an electrical meter (left) adds joy to our experience of a public space.

Thus, there are no secluded hot tubs under a gazebo here. What happens at the private/public edge makes an urban village and is the focus of this book.

Comfort: measure of an urban village

As "man is the measure of the world," so human comfort is the measure of a city.

My own experience with local government is as a staff member, citizen, and developer, and I believe our society makes the problem of city building far too complicated. We confuse it with grandeur and we confuse it with complex public administration. It is neither. The main task is making people comfortable, the same task faced by the host at a party. In fact, think of the main job for the city planner as being, say, the Amy Vanderbilt or Miss Manners of the city.

All around us are examples of excellence in concept and design: city comforts. They are simple to recognize, simple to explain, and, by and large, simple to build. These designs-that-work can be repeated many times before, if ever, they run thin.

Density is a *by-product* of creating interesting places

There is almost universal fear of the deleterious impacts of urban sprawl, and much hope for what is perceived as its opposite: urban villages. The urban village implies "densification" — more people living in a given area. But the word "densification" lacks poetic, much less political, appeal. Certainly zoning changes to allow higher residential density are a necessary component of any central city or urban village strategy.

But allowing higher densities is only a precursor and it can put the cart before the horse. Discussions of densification often implicitly assume that people must be cajoled into higher-density housing. Though there is an element of truth to that, the cajoling that must take place is in the form of creating great neighborhoods.

People are quite willing, even extremely willing, to live in high density if the amenity value of the surrounding environment is also great. Condominiums and apartments on the waterfront, any waterfront, attract people. So do views. People will clamor to live in an interesting, walkable, human-scaled neighborhood.

One of the trade-offs (and benefits) of purchasing in a multifamily structure in a dense neighborhood should be that one can walk in safety and comfort to stores, restaurants, theaters, and so forth along pleasant public sidewalks. Such pedestrian-friendly environments are called for by the public policy of many jurisdictions, but we are lagging in actually creating them. Moreover, and even more troubling, we seem to be incapable of managing the public spaces of the pedestrian-friendly neighborhoods that already exist.

A decline in the quality of life in higher-density neighborhoods exacerbates the preference for the single-family house. The detached dwelling offers the home buyer the opportunity to create a private zone of comfort. Even if the public space of the immediate block or neighborhood declines, the house owner has his/her lot on which to buffer the world.

The buyer in a multifamily environment must deal with the high "transaction costs" of condominium association decision-making: many committees and many rules. There is limited opportunity to enrich the environment because the open space of most multifamily structures is limited and held in common.

Multifamily dwellers are thus forced to take on the task of improving their neighborhood environment in the public space of the sidewalks and streets. They are ill equipped for this task and face enormous institutional resistance from local municipal bureaucracies, most of which are still rooted in the task of moving automobiles. It is not uncommon for fifty percent of an American city's land area to be in public right-of-way, but most of that is devoted to cars. But in that public space is the greatest possibility of small (and relatively inexpensive) improvements that can increase neighborhood comfort. These small city comforts have the potential to benefit a neighborhood well beyond their cost. But they are very difficult for homeowners to carry out.

Over the past twenty years, and in general, the rate of increase in value of multifamily condominiums has lagged behind single-family houses. I believe that is because people are aware (unconsciously and not) that they will have less control over their neighborhood. Since the basic lesson of home buying is to "buy neighborhood," this is a bad portent for the future of sustainable cities in which multifamily housing is expected to play a large part.

The way to densification is indirect. It is to propel local government (or to allow private property owners the ability) to create public environments that can compete in quality of life with what one finds in single-family neighborhoods.

That means adhering to a few simple rules of urban design — the Three Rules — and encouraging a host of city comforts.

Boston, MA

Why mixed-use? Creating connections

Mixed-use is typically associated with the neighborly urban village. Mixed-use has become one of the mantras of progressive urban planning. The urban village will indeed have a mixture of uses within close walking distance of each other — or even down a flight of stairs. But why?

The purpose of mixing uses, allowing different activities to rub cheek by jowl, is to foster more complex and intertwined human relations and thus more interesting places. The purpose is to help create human connections — not to mix activities per se. There is nothing magic about mixing uses.

Particularly since World War II it has been planning dogma to separate uses. The gentler and quieter residential districts should be protected from the busier commercial and industrial uses. Most contemporary land-use laws focus on buffering "weaker" uses from the impacts of stronger and incompatible uses. These concerns are based on common sense and are antique. The Mesopotamians, for example, forbade metal workers from plying their trade within cities because of danger from fire and smoke. Even within contemporary higher-density areas, resistance to mixed-use should not be tossed off as bourgeois decadency; there are inherent conflicts between, for example, residences for families with young children and a tavern oriented to people in their twenties. To a point, separation of conflicting uses makes sense (see Chapter 10 on buffers). But taken to an extreme it has led to vast monocultures of uses.

North Vancouver, BC, Canada

Mixing can be valuable. Ecosystems are richest at their edges, where habitats and species overlap. Mixed-use neighborhoods are often more resilient, stimulating, and interesting than single-use neighborhoods. Hybrid vigor is recognized in agronomy; mixture of uses can also impart vigor to social communities.

Some activities conflict in natural systems; some uses come to prevail. So too in human systems. Some uses do conflict with each other — housing wants quiet; shopping thrives on bustle. But they can coexist close together if their conflict points are identified. For example, parking for residential and commercial tenants in mixed-use buildings can have separate entrances to diminish noise and security problems.

Mixed-use might make sense at transportation hubs. It is logical to put daily shopping where you change mode of transport. It's convenient. Instead of taking the bus home and then driving to shop, one can shop in the course of returning from work.

Of course the single-family neighborhood will continue to be the staple of settlement through the foreseeable future. But even in such areas, low-key commercial uses can fit in and add vitality, economic stability, and even safety because they add people to the daytime population.

CHAPTER 2

BUMPING INTO PEOPLE

Cities — especially urban villages — are about bumping into old friends and making new friends. Or they should be. The city's job is to bring people together.

The sign at right shows the heart of the urban problem. It is hauntingly located near a high bridge.

For adults, the problem of the city is alienation, districts without community, without a friendly and familiar face.

The Three Rules, which I summarize on the back cover and will discuss in detail shortly, exist to create cities

Portland, OR

and neighborhoods conducive to bumping into people. Their purpose is not to further some architectural theory but to encourage human connections through serendipitous interaction.

Early cities started as trade hubs, military centers, or religious shrines. Cities still flourish for the same reasons. For each, the city provides a place of contact. The city is a place to make a business deal, enact rules and regulations, make friends, and even fall in love. The city is a place to communicate.

The possibility of the accidental meeting is what makes the city a fertile place. From the chance conversation springs the new business idea. People position themselves in cities so as to be able to make contact with others who have common interests. But our cities work far below their potential. They fail to encourage the unplanned and serendipitous encounter upon which business grows.

Modern cities work even less well for pleasure. As Christopher Alexander puts it, cities are a mechanism for "sustaining human contact." He says, "People come to cities for contact. That's what cities are: meeting places. Yet the people who live in cities are often contactless and alienated. A few of them are physically lonely: almost all of them live in a state of endless inner loneliness. They have thousands of contacts, but the contacts are empty and unsatisfying."

People flee cities when they fail as places where casual contact can flourish and create a sense of community. The modern city falls short in providing environments for communication. Sociologist Ray Oldenburg calls these environments "third places" in his book *The Great Good Place*. He describes the first two places as the home and the workplace. The third place is where one bumps into friends and neighbors in an unplanned manner. Such a place is a public place: the bar, the pub, the coffee shop, the deli. Food or drink is essential; so is proximity to the home. But modern America is short of such places.

Ponder the '90s TV show *Cheers*, which takes place in a tavern of the same name. Its theme song fondly and plaintively describes the tavern as a place "where everybody knows your name." It speaks volumes about our current civilization that a place where one is recognized as an individual is something unusual enough to merit mentioning in a popular song.

We speak constantly of neighborhoods and community. But without the third place — the commons outside the home and workplace, where people stumble into each other and where your name is known — we do not have a neighborhood but simply an area.

Of course public authorities should not and will not go into the tavern business. But the following principles can help create public places more conducive to meeting people, and they are courtesies that should be no surprise to the Amy Vanderbilts of the city.

Santa Barbara, CA

Santa Barbara, CA

Cannon Beach, OR

St. Helena, CA

Provide seats

A seat is an explicit invitation to stay, either with others or by oneself.

Unfortunately, because of concern that the "wrong" people, i.e., street people, will be the ones to use public seats, too often such seats are removed. It would be naive to assert that some street people present no problem, and it would be heartless to deny any social responsibility for the homeless. The wise social policy about them is far beyond the scope of this book. But removing public seating does not solve the problem: it only denies the rest of the population its due of an inviting city.

Let people purchase food or drink

It seems inevitable that people at almost every party will end up in the kitchen. Oh, perhaps not at the White House or the Elysée Palace, but at pretty much every party where they feel comfortable, they'll end up in the kitchen, around the food. The same principle applies in public: eating together connects us, and a good meal is always the start to a seduction or a contract or a peace agreement. Let us break bread together. Allow and encourage food service that provides seating adjacent to or even on the sidewalk.

Even at a mountain resort, people like to hang around the food.

Boston, MA

Sisters, OR

Vancouver, BC, Canada

Nefertiti Beach, Green River, UT

Offer a conversation piece

Every host and hostess knows that it's nice to have some odd objects lying about for people to notice, exclaim over, and discuss. It's best if the object is a souvenir from one's last trip to Tokyo or Tibet, but it really doesn't matter. The purpose is to divert attention from "I and thou" and to place it on some external object. Third parties are always popular as a subject, but we call that gossip, and that's risky for strangers (not knowing who is who).

In public places, as on the beach, art engages people and always does nicely to help open a conversation by providing an external object on which to focus.

Do it discreetly

Fostering social interaction is difficult, and an overly enthusiastic or match-making host or hostess can be the surest way to spoil a burgeoning conversation. ("You two will love each other: you have so much in common!" Or "Aren't we all having fun!?")

Caution to planners

Be limited in your goals. Creating community — which is what all this boils down to — is a worthy goal. But it is a goal largely beyond the reach of government.

Community evolves from individual conversations. Venues for these conversations are difficult to create. That's one reason very few adults ever hang around the so-called community center. Such places, built and managed by bureaucracy, most often fall flat. Necessarily run by gray government, they lack the unique and quirky personality often contributed by individual enterprise. Interesting public spaces provide only a framework, with the daily details supplied by aware entrepreneurs who recognize what is working and what is not, and act immediately.

Seattle, WA
photo by Fred Housel

Put public space in the sun

The sun is the prime mover and the source of all life on earth. There is science-fiction speculation that life might be able to evolve with another energy source and in the absence of solar radiation. But we are earthlings, and we are all drawn to the sun. Like most animals, such as these elk, we like to gather in the sun in groups.

Thus, if you would like a public plaza to be used, place it on a side of the building where it will receive sunlight. This may seem elementary, but it is still often ignored.

Better to have too much sun than too little. Shade may be needed in extreme climates, or for a few days a year in the temperate zones. But shade can be provided with awnings and trellises. It is much more difficult to bend the sunshine to the north side of the building if that's where you placed the plaza.

Banff, AB, Canada

Nantucket, MA

Encourage the chance encounter

Chance encounter. It could be the name of a movie from the 1930s. But it is the most basic work of a city. Many interesting things happen to us because we bump into someone by accident: new projects, new clients, and new love affairs. Cities provide a venue for these serendipitous and accidental meetings. The city gives us the opportunity to plan to be in a place where accidents can happen, where we can run into others.

For a brief moment in the 1990s, there was a notion afoot that electronic cyberspace would obviate the need for cities. "We'll all do our work in front of our console from our home office" was a cliche. And even if we don't work at home, maybe we will shop from there. Physical proximity will not be needed. The purpose of the city will vanish in a flood of electrons. The virtual office and virtual store via Internet will replace bricks and mortar. Such predictions have obviously failed. Of course it was always impossible for people in construction to work in cyberspace. Information workers can live and work far from each other. But I think that it is generally accepted that people prefer to go to a place where they can see others.

In the traditional office the watercooler is the place where people meet accidentally. The virtual office would have succeeded if it had a virtual watercooler. But it didn't, and the momentary dream of telecommuting, even in the face of crushing traffic congestion, has failed. People like to go to work for its sociability.

Cities, which still face challenges from suburban expansion, should pay attention to this desire for social contact. Cities successful in facing this challenge will recognize the importance to economic growth of social interaction and chance meetings. In every possible way, from convention centers to the design of sidewalks, cities that are designed to be sociable will be at an advantage in the economy of the future.

The future of cities lies in the possibility they offer for the chance encounter.

Even something as simple as the sidewalk bazaar can contribute to the city of accidental meetings.

Build neighborhoods for the social stroll

People like to walk together.

In many parts of the world, particularly the Latin nations, it is a part of daily life to take an evening stroll. There is a complex and involved ritual to this walk, this promenade, this *passaggiaeta* or *paseo*, as it's called in Italy and Spain. It was a tradition in France and Britain, and in the United States, too, before the automobile spread us so far apart that now one has to drive to find a place to walk.

Certain groups only walk with each other; men walk in some manner; women in another, perhaps; children, teenagers, and the very old in yet more ways. It all depends on the specific town and its customs. The stroll starts and stops with invisible but predictable regularity. The *passaggiaeta* is good for the health, but it is more a social exercise than anything else. Chatting, watching other people, and being watched are the reasons for the social stroll.

Tokyo, Japan
photo by Hiromitsu Yajima

In the U.S. we have teenagers cruising in cars. Older people use the shopping malls for their promenade. The stroll is a universal custom and impulse, though an impulse largely thwarted by the design of our American cities.

But suppose one had the opportunity to lay out a new town or merely a new suburban subdivision or perhaps just revitalize a shopping district and wished to meet the demand of future residents to take part in this ancient tradition. How would one proceed?

To a remarkable degree, we do have that opportunity. Suburban development still proceeds apace, and there are many, many plats (divisions of streets, blocks, and lots) and new towns now on the drawing boards, so there are plenty of chances to do things differently and more traditionally.

Here are a few rules for walkways suited to the social stroll.

- *Continuity*: Create a path that forms a continuous loop, such as around a square or a small pond. People of all ages generally prefer to walk in a loop, which gives a sense of departure and arrival. Furthermore, it is important that the route be clear, routine, and "automatic" enough so that decisions about which way to turn are unneeded and hence can never interrupt the conversation.
- *Length*: The path must not be too lengthy so that people may pass each other more than once. Flirting can't be hurried. One must be able to make eye contact, remake it, and then remake it again in order for the social contact to take root.
- *Width*: It would be ideal for the path to be wide enough for two groups to pass each other without awkward rearrangements to interrupt the conversation.

Bryant Park, New York, NY
photo by Christopher K. Leman

Put your cards (or chess pieces) on the table

People enjoy the amusement and challenge of board games. They are engaging and fun. But such distractions are a staple of culture for a deeper reason: they allow easy and nonthreatening socializing, with the enormous exception of the temptation to cheat. But cheating aside, card and board games provide an opportunity to be with people for hours and hours, actually enjoying their company, with nary a word of consequence ever spoken. There is no obligation to make conversation or, worse, to become ensnared in a pointless and unpleasant argument on politics, religion, money, sex, or any of the other aspects of life that are so interesting and that can divide us most disagreeably.

Cannon Beach, OR

Build close to the sidewalk

One of the benefits of smaller scale is that conversation is encouraged simply by physical proximity. People don't have to raise their voices if they are sitting close to the sidewalk.

Not incidentally, seating close to the sidewalk is good for business; the power of suggestion can work on the passerby who sees customers enjoying what they have bought.

This scale is often called human scale. What does that mean?

One useful definition of human scale is a functional one. For example: an apartment building in which a child on the sidewalk can converse with his/her mother at a window up above. That is human scale: a place where the ability to have a conversation is allowed by the very size of the space.

Note: The town in Oregon where I took this picture has approximately eighty benches in its four blocks of main street. That's seating for about four hundred people: a superb seating-to-sidewalk ratio. It is a very comfortable town.

Queenstown, New Zealand

Bellingham, WA

Gather 'round the hearth

Everyone has been to a party in a large house in which by 11 P.M. the "living" rooms are empty and the guests are all crammed together in the kitchen. Such is the power of the hearth.

Create something similar in public spaces, such as at this shopping mall (above) or outside this restaurant.

Seattle, WA
photo by Fred Housel

Provide a place for music

These entry steps to a major office building function well in several ways. Of course, access to the building is their first function. They also act as a viewpoint to observe the passing scene.

But their circular shape also creates a small amphitheater and a place for performance, particularly music. This small space is adjacent to but off a bustling sidewalk. Musicians (either street or school) can play here without inconveniencing passersby who do not care to stop to listen.

Noontime concerts (called the Out to Lunch Series in Seattle) add music to daily life. Music is an unobtrusive way to bring people together. It soothes. It helps us while away boring times. It is an ancient pathway to religious and community experience.

Bainbridge Island, WA

Reclaim and people the parking lot

The entrance to a supermarket is an ideal place to sell potted plants and cut flowers. It is also ideal for selling newspapers, which of course leads to espresso,

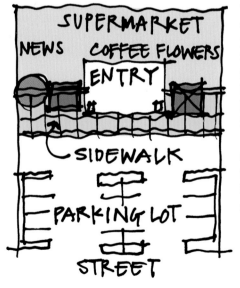

without which a newspaper would be dry indeed. But what good is a newspaper and a morning drink without a table and chair? So soon enough there is a new hangout, an ongoing liveliness to make the parking lot more human, and an additional attraction for the store's customers.

The informal series of open roof and tents was so successful that since this photo was taken the arrangement has been formalized with a more permanent all-weather structure.

Seattle, WA

Build bus shelters with public services

Large terminals often have shops and services — consider Grand Central Station — so why not make the small stop more pleasant?

Some transit stops are too small — with too few riders — to support any services at all. But surely a number of bus stops generate enough pedestrian traffic to support an espresso bar, newspaper and magazine kiosk, bank machine, flower shop, shoe-shine stand, video rental in the larger ones, or at the very least a public telephone.

The transportation authority might build a kiosk with a "pop-out" end so entrepreneurs could plug in their own self-contained gear. The authority should not have to do too much: utility lines would be sufficient. The authority might be paid a percentage rent to reflect excellent locations. The successful retailer would inevitably gain the status of informant on bus schedules, lost dogs and cats, and general watchkeeper.

Seattle, WA

Use sound to permit conversation

Not only spies but ordinary folks can benefit from "white noise" to give them privacy. This park is located on a harsh urban corner where no one would want to spend much time chatting. Yet the background of the roaring waterfall provides a little bit of pastoral peace and creates privacy for conversation.

Seattle, WA
photo by Barbara Gray

Promote growing

The urge to plant and cultivate is deep but not easily satisfied if you have no ground of your own. P-Patches are common ground where people can lease their own patch of dirt (typically from a city agency) and gain support from others. It is in such informal places that neighbors can meet and the practical wisdom of older people can be passed along.

Seattle, WA

Allow strangers to sit together

Some out-of-town restaurateurs came to visit. They praised one restaurant highly and complimented the proprietor. "It's awesome! We love it! The only thing you've got to change are the tables. They are too big. They're big enough for twelve!" The proprietor smiled. Without the large tables, his restaurant wouldn't be a neighborhood hangout.

To join a stranger at a restaurant table for two or four is, for Americans, a very forward act. It is an aggressive and committing gesture, unless the seat is the last one in the house and one can point to the excuse of necessity.

But to sit down at a common table (when there are nothing but common tables) where a stranger is already sitting, is nothing at all except playing by house rules. To make an idle remark to that stranger, to which he or she can casually respond or just as casually decline, is nothing out of the ordinary and, for shy people, a more comfortable engagement.

The great abyss of urban loneliness is bridged by the large table of this restaurant, this "third place," and such casual contact is what cities are all about.

The only warning: such community tables are a public place, albeit small. They are not the place to propose marriage, interview for a job, or negotiate the "big deal."

Another danger: such third-place socializing becomes addictive.

Seattle, WA

Build in bus stop seating

This modest gesture to the street is well used by neighbors waiting for the bus. (It was being used, in fact; but the photographer was shy and waited for riders to board their bus before shooting.)

The landlord lost some rentable square footage, but the neighborhood gained a speck of sheltered repose.

Seattle, WA

Create public spaces simply with seats

Seats of any kind are an invitation and an announcement: "This is a public space. Sit down and give your brain a rest." It doesn't take much. One can create a public realm by simply giving people the opportunity to sit and linger.

Seattle, WA

Quench the thirst for community

The physical surroundings of this corner are every bit as barren and unfriendly as they appear.

Yet the urban thirst for new experiences and stimulation is so great (and obvious to all) that even here in an urban Sahara the entrepreneur can — with the most minimal investment — create an oasis for people to hang out, meet people, swap ideas — as the stand's sidewalk board (to the right) proposes.

Like the lichen — which pioneers the barest and most inhospitable mountain summit and gradually, through its own chemical action, breaks down the hardest rock into soil where plants can grow — the espresso bar creates a fertile ground for community.

Again, government action can thwart such small improvements as this espresso bar. But its creation — so very vital to the real life of cities — is beyond institutional reach.

Seattle, WA

Seattle, WA
photo by Barbara Gray

Use movable chairs

Communities are not announced by planners but emerge out of places that people make their own. Spaces to sit and chat allow such ownership to develop. People gain such a sense of ownership by lingering at a spot.

Enliven a sterile plaza with tables and chairs. They are inexpensive, flexible, and allow the users to program the space on a short-term basis. People can rearrange them to face into or away from the sun and wind, to avoid noise, to better hear one another, to accommodate the larger group, or to provide privacy for the couple or individual.

William Whyte, the observer of public space, observed that there is an inescapable ritual of sitting down. As the sitter takes a chair, she shifts it — if only a few inches — and in doing so she exerts her territoriality, making the space more her own. A space becomes more meaningful when people are allowed to create this personal and temporary territoriality with movable chairs. One might fear the hassle and property loss from loose seating, but the comfort level is worth the cost.

Portland, OR

Let readers sip

A welcome trend in bookstores (now a delightful cliche) is to allow customers to eat and drink (once the book or magazine has been bought, of course).

"Oh! Is that the new issue of _____? Anything good in it?"

The magazine or book, its cover quite visible, acts like a state's sign at a political convention, bringing together those of like inclination and interest.

As yet another illustration of the tumultuous pace of change in today's world, the current trend is to provide wireless Internet access in coffee bars. As I read on the Web edition of *The New York Times*:

Ms. Kachouh, who used to work in a Starbucks in Union Square where she said the clientele consisted entirely of office workers and tourists, said many of her regulars work at home. They include writers, psychologists, psychiatrists, lawyers and others. Accordingly, she said, she had recently arranged for wireless Internet access for the store.

"I have all these people who need it," she said sympathetically. "It's too hot for them to work at home."

But did she really want tables tied up for hours?

"It's good," she said. "The busier I look, the busier I get."

CHAPTER 3

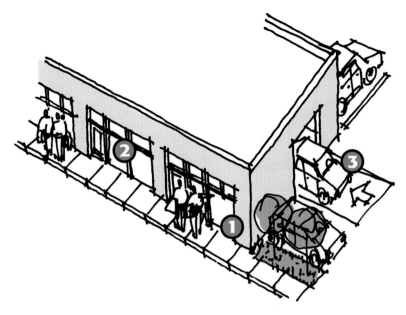

THE THREE RULES

This is the most important chapter in this book. If the problem is to create a walkable, pedestrian-oriented neighborhood, much of the answer is architectural. Actually, it is not so much "architectural" in the usual sense of the word, for it ignores style. Site plan trumps architecture. That means the basic arrangement of the building on the site is far more important than what usually passes for architecture: the exterior appearance and "envelope" of the structure.

This chapter explains the Three Rules for creating such places. Let's assume that we agree that the goal is to create this mythical urban village. How do we do it?

The key decision is the position of the building with respect to the sidewalk. This decision determines whether you have a city or a suburb.

1 Build to the sidewalk (i.e., property line).

2 Make the building front "permeable" (i.e., no blank walls).

3 Prohibit parking lots in front of the building.

BUILDING
SIDEWALK
STREET

The decision is a very simple one: place the building alongside the sidewalk. That's it. Don't make it complicated. Simply bring the building to the sidewalk. The banal and all too typical strip center below could have contributed to a pedestrian neighborhood had it been designed to work with the Rules rather than against them.

If you question this, consider the places that most people like to go on vacation: New York, Paris, London, Aspen, Carmel, Nantucket, Park City, Friday Harbor, and even Disneyland. Every last one of them is built so that the building walls are right next to the sidewalk.

Historically, with only human and animal power to move goods, and with market forces in charge, it made sense to bring the building close to the street in the effort to maximize profit, creating, ironically for modern, often anticapitalist preservationists, the most charming streets.

Seattle, WA

Los Angeles, CA

The Rules are only a start

The Three Rules will emerge over and over again in this book. Their importance cannot be overemphasized; they are the common denominator and *leit-motiv* of comfortable urban spaces. They are an absolute necessity and precursor to creating pedestrian-oriented communities. But by themselves they are insufficient. There are unhealthy, inner-city neighborhoods that follow them. There are auto-dominated — but healthy — suburbs that don't. But as a general rule the Three Rules are essential to create human settlements that have any real sense of interpersonal community.

RULE 1:
Build to the sidewalk
(i.e., property line)

Create a strong "streetwall" in which each building meets or comes close to the sidewalk. The sidewalk is important because it channels pedestrian movements and forces people into closer proximity where they may bump into each other and act neighborly.

Obviously we don't want to end up with streetfronts like this one at the right, but as a way of deconstructing a desirable streetfront, and to make our point clear, we start with this rule.

(A note on terms: In the majority of situations and for practical purposes, the sidewalk is at the property line.)

As we said before, this rule is central, and to paraphrase Professor William Strunk, Jr. (in *The Elements of Style*), whose desire to eliminate useless words left him repeating the useful ones for emphasis: "Build to the sidewalk! Build to the sidewalk! Build to the sidewalk!"

Seattle, WA

SUB-RULE: Locate the inside floor level as close as possible to the level of the sidewalk outside.

Make it easy to see and move into the building. Current laws on accommodating people with disabilities encourage this anyway, but don't let the ramp be the only method. Try to keep the interior floor levels as close to the sidewalk grade as possible. To the right we see the exception to the rule, which is acceptable only because it is a retrofit of an old townhouse. It works in a historic context, but it is not ideal.

Boston, MA

Vancouver, BC, Canada

RULE 2:
Make the building front "permeable" (i.e., no blank walls)

Connect the inside of the building and the sidewalk outside with windows and doors.

Life attracts life. If you can't see the merchandise for sale or the other patrons mingling, you won't stop to go in. It's a basic rule of retailing and practical urban design the world over. Flaunt it. Don't hide it with a blank wall. Place windows and openings along the sidewalk.

Of course, not only must people be able to see in and out, they must also be able to enter. Therefore put your front doors where they are visible from and directly face the sidewalk.

Making the building open to the sidewalk is a common denominator of all healthy neighborhoods and potential urban villages.

SUB-RULE: Prohibit mirrored glass or window coverings that block visibility.

Creating connections between humans inside the building and outside it is the essence of creating pedestrian-oriented streets. So it follows that mirrored glass, or blinds, or any other device to block visibility is a rule breaker, as would be mirrored sunglasses in a tête-à-tête. If you have experienced the discomfort of talking with someone wearing mirrored sunglasses, which deliberately limit contact, you understand what I mean. No matter what advantage it might otherwise offer, such as energy savings or privacy, blocking visibility is inimical to a pedestrian-oriented street.

Seattle, WA

RULE 3:
Prohibit parking lots in front of the building

Put on-site parking lots above, below, behind, or beside. Pedestrian-oriented neighborhoods start with location of the parking lot.

Parking lots are a necessity. But unless you are in high school, or are at a tailgate party before a football game, or at a classic car *concours d'elegance*, parking lots are not the place you want to hang around. It is ironic, of course: we invest such great money and emo-

Seattle, WA

tion in our cars and yet we don't want to hang around them in parking lots.

Parking lots are crucial; taming them will be one of the challenges of piecing together urban villages.

In an urban village, there are no parking lots along the streetfront. This is the corollary of the rule that asks for the buildings to be brought to the sidewalk. Since it's so important (and so simple) it bears repeating: locate on-site parking above, below, behind through an alley, behind from a street, or beside the building, and place the building at the sidewalk. *Save the front for people.*

Vancouver, BC, Canada

parking above the building

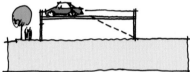

Vancouver, BC, Canada

parking below the building

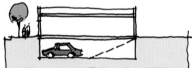

Boulder, CO

parking behind through an alley

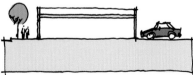

parking behind from a street

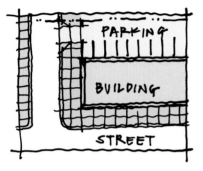

Seattle, WA

parking beside the building

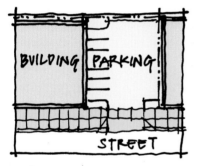

Seattle, WA

The rule applies at every scale. This small mixed-use building (below right) is on a site with no alley. Required parking can be provided only if cars are allowed to cross the sidewalk. It's not the ideal, but in the parking context of this city (every building must have its own parking) there was no alternative. The entry is minimized and the front still has commercial space facing the street.

Another solution might have been to relieve the developer of parking requirements entirely in lieu of contributing to a neighborhood parking garage or lot — see page 88.

Seattle, WA

White Rock, BC, Canada

Even large corporations can follow rules about the location of the parking lot, even though often there is resistance and claims of "We can't operate that way." Here is a large supermarket that has underground parking (albeit within a shopping center, but it could very well have been within an urban core). The problem of vertical movement of shoppers with their carts — it's a common question — is solved simply with an escalator (or elevator).

White Rock, BC, Canada

SUB-RULE: Allow on-street parking. Stop-and-go parking is essential to real shopping districts.

These are very simple rules but, alas, in reality easier said than done. The reality is that in our car-oriented culture there are situations in which we want the parking very close at hand. The typical strip-mall approach — the parking in front of the building — is hard to avoid if you want to serve people late at night.

Talk as we might about proper urban design, no one is going to feel comfortable going to a convenience store at 2 A.M. and walking around from the back of the building to the entrance. It's bad enough when the parking is in front — in the dark of night it is not an inviting choice. The basic rules of feeling safe — natural surveillance and territoriality — are at work in the conventional strip-center development. But while this principle may work for the one site, the same pattern, repeated over and over, is counterproductive to safety as it creates a neighborhood where people only want to be in cars.

Luckily, there are very few places such as the twenty-four-hour convenience store where access at odd hours must be a design constraint. The sketch at the right shows an alternative to parking lots between the street and the storefront. Certainly safety is essential. But the idea that parking must be in front of the shop, right off the sidewalk, would be designing a city around a worst-case situation. It would create a city designed around the need to go to a convenience store

Nantucket, MA

Seattle, WA

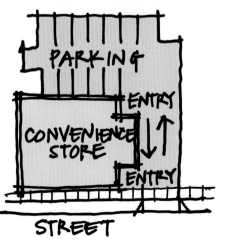

for a six-pack at 2 A.M. So the basic rule must be to put the parking out of sight. (Here is where we see the importance of on-street parking.)

A comfortable city starts with the location of the parking lot. To paraphrase Mies van der Rohe, form follows parking.

The primacy of parking requirements in zoning codes supports that statement. But so does the process of design. The very first step in designing — from a hut to a high-rise — is to figure out how to get the car onto and off the site and where to store it.

Our three rules simply acknowledge that process. We accept the centrality of parking but ask that it be done in a manner that supports rather than destroys pedestrian-oriented streets.

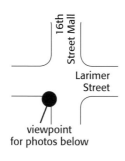

The pastiche below shows the power of the Three Rules. The photos were taken from the same spot. On the left we have a lively, pedestrian-oriented street; on the right we have an incomplete following of the Three Rules that yields a sterile and lonely streetfront.

And it could have been avoided had the builders of the building on the right understood the Rules and designed the parking garage (see page 187) to be a contributor to the street rather than an enemy.

Denver, CO

Here is another example of the power of the Three Rules to shape places, even in the face of global enterprise. The KFC, so familiar to North Americans, nestles into Queenstown, New Zealand. It provides a streetfront and yet it also provides the drive-through access demanded by auto-oriented cultures.

Whether this compromise is acceptable is up to local communities. One can certainly argue that the Rules should be inviolate. But the reality of land-use politics sometimes calls for compromise.

It may seem pretty deflating that great streetscapes can be based on such simple elements as the Three Rules. After all, shouldn't it be more complicated, artistic, requiring a heightened sensibility and aesthetic? That would be nice for snobs. But great cooks often say that the basis of great cuisine is simply fresh food. So it is with great streets. The irreducible basis is simple: the Three Rules.

Queenstown, New Zealand

Queenstown, New Zealand

Photo by Bryan H. Smith

Be the hedgehog, not the fox

The English philosopher Isaiah Berlin made famous a quote from an ancient Greek poet: "The fox knows many things, but the hedgehog knows one big thing."

This thought serves us well in urban planning. The Three Rules are the "one big thing" we must follow to create pedestrian-oriented neighborhoods. Even when rebuffed by large institutional forces such as the big-box store, the state highway department, or the nonprofit institution, the Three Rules focus the discussion on the few key variables that really count to create pedestrian-oriented streetscapes.

Such creation happens in an explicitly political arena, with interest groups and lobbying. Around every regulatory body such as a planning agency gathers the regulated interests and those concerned. The U.S. Forest Service has the timber companies and the environmental groups. The corollary is that supporters of comfortable cities must have a set of easy-to-grasp mental tools and standards by which to judge new development. I believe that the Three Rules provide such a framework. They are simple to understand and go to the heart of the issue in creating walkable neighborhoods. They pick out a key relationship and work it thoroughly. Most "amateurs" (and it is no disrespect to characterize most mayors and councilmembers as nonspecialists when it comes to urban design and planning) face issues for which their education and prior work provide little insight.

The Three Rules provide an analytic framework that can be easily visualized to help create walkable streets.

Some developers know the rules

People who build ersatz cities also understand that this spatial relationship is central to our sense of being in a city. There is a very interesting tourist attraction called CityWalk: it is a festival shopping center, a place to shop for things one doesn't need.

Of course it has valet parking, which is de rigueur in Los Angeles. Valet parking combines both status and security. Only uniformed attendants are allowed in the parking structure. The attendants run to and fro to fetch cars. Anyone else in the garage sticks out by their presence alone.

The fascinating thing about CityWalk is that its developers understood the essence of "citiness": it is buildings that come up to sidewalks where people can stroll and shop safely. This mall — even more than most malls — has the basic village pattern: the old village sidewalk. While many developers seem to have an aversion to cities, they also recognize that people are drawn to city-like situations and will drive to find them.

Los Angeles, CA

Boulder, CO

It's a very plastic world

What is meant by "plastic" is that our cities are undergoing constant change. They may look solid and fixed. But over even a very short period of years, they undergo enormous reconstruction, a characteristic of a vibrant economy.

We can take advantage of this process of regeneration by applying the Three Rules to every land-use action on a commercial street. Here is an example that arose out of the natural desire of the property owner to maximize value from an old supermarket. He divided the very deep (120 feet) store in half so that what had once been the back of a large supermarket — blank and uninviting — is opened up with storefronts and becomes a new front to the street. It's not ideal that the shops are so far above street grade, but that was the existing condition.

ORIGINAL SUPERMARKET STORE FRONT

120 FT.

NEW SHOPS 60 FT. / 60 FT.

⌐ MAKE NEW STOREFRONTS AT 'BACK'

Edmonton, AB, Canada

The problem of the arterial

On a larger site often found at an urban edge, one can place the parking within, creating a strong street edge and yet providing the required on-site parking.

Major urban arterials are often controlled by state highway departments. There is a difficult push and pull between the local government's desire to transform an auto-oriented strip (see page 7, "Dystopia") into something at least a little bit better and the state highway department's mandate to move as many cars through the area as possible. On-street parking is usually impossible, at least at peak commuter hours.

One solution is to create a street wall of shops while allowing parking on the inside.

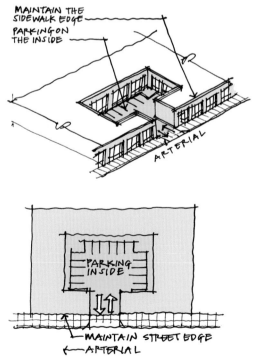

Salt Lake City, UT

The special problem of the major institution

Do the Three Rules have any place with noncommercial buildings? Or on "campuses"? Yes.

Public (federal, state, local, special district, etc.) and nonprofit (museums, hospitals, universities, etc.) institutions develop a huge amount of urban property. They have a significant impact on the urban environment. They often have a strong institutional ambition and wish to both manifest and further that identity in architectural form. While the institution might do great work, its urge to differentiate itself and show itself as unique architecturally can be very destructive to the streetscape.

Typically, an institutional design symbolizes its uniqueness in two related ways:

- *By use of sheer space (i.e., distance)*. Often, as if to mimic the English gentleman who recoils from trade, their designers hew to the image of "the campus": pulled back from the city and its jostling activity into a plaza or park.
- *By use of style to separate the building from its surroundings*. Each building is a self-proclaimed work of genius by a "star" architect, whose name is too well known and too fleeting of fame to justify mentioning here. Such an "object" building is separated from its neighbors by outrageous stylistic gimmicks and often setbacks from the sidewalk to form a purposefully symbolic urban moat.

Cambridge, MA

Some people, of course, do see cities as collections of architectural sculptures, as "precious objects." Much of what passes for public commentary on the built environment contends with such faddish work. Indeed there is much to appreciate, in an amusement park manner, in such buildings. A few such are indeed a lively leavening, an exception — a raisin in the oatmeal: contributing most when rare — to create variety and draw attention to the few buildings that symbolize the community. The city hall on the opposite page appropriately and firmly states its importance in its city. But imagine if every institution were able to speak so loudly.

But the "precious object" school leads to cities of isolation. While the sylvan campus and its urban progeny, the precious object, cannot be faulted in their own place, their own place is rarely in the city. Campuses — even when they have a green edge — attempt to isolate themselves from their surrounding neighborhood. Even when the campus grows and sites at the formal campus edge are developed, the building often faces inward.

Our key task is to ensure that the exception does not devour the rule. Object buildings set on an isolated podium cannot create an urban context. I don't mean to be overly dogmatic and insist that literally every building in a city must adhere to the Three Rules. In fact, only ninety-seven to ninety-eight percent of buildings in commercial zones should follow the rules. We should always allow for the exceptional building, the precious object.

Seattle, WA

To create pedestrian-oriented neighborhoods almost all noncommercial build-ings should adhere to the Three Rules and relate to the street around them. The goal should be to create "background buildings" that fit into the cityscape and do not call attention to themselves.

The photo on the previous page shows an institutional building at Harvard Square that acts as part of the community. There are shops on the plaza and one can walk through it to an adjoining street. (The reader familiar with the build-ing will quickly interject, "But that building doesn't strictly adhere to the Three Rules." True enough. The response is simple: an occasional plaza is acceptable so long as the default position is to follow the Three Rules.)

Other institutions can be even bolder in following the Rules. Aside from buildings that require high security such as "justice centers" (police and courts), almost all institutions have functions that could be at street level.

Here, in the photo above, is an excellent solution for a symphony hall, a use that inherently does not need, much less even want, any direct contact with the street. Its foyer runs the full length of the block and provides an assembly point for concertgoers. It also provides space for refreshments during the day. While strict, the Three Rules do not need to be an oppressive and limiting force. In fact, once their centrality and importance to the creation of streetscapes are grasped, they offer a central focus and constraint through which design imagination can soar.

Portland, OR

The inevitable cry: "There's no demand for retail space"

The Three Rules are a distillation of what actually works to make interesting places. They are a *post hoc* observation rather than an *a priori* conjecture. And they imply mixed-used neighborhoods of residential-above-retail. The politics of development of such neighborhoods is inevitably, or at least often, accompanied by developers' assertions that there is no demand for more retail space. Such is often true. Moreover, development firms rarely have expertise across several markets, such as housing *and* retail. So there is often resistance to mixed-use because the technical as well as political know-how is not found in the same firm, adding to the perceived risk.

Planning authorities must address such concerns with sympathy and practicality so that requirements for retail space at ground level are in tune with neighborhood demands.

But two points need to be made.

- *The retail space may be very shallow.* In fact (see page 212, showing an urban design tool), it is only the edge of the building where it meets the sidewalk that is at issue, perhaps the first fifteen to thirty feet. A very shallow space can be accommodated and yet provide vitality to the street.

- *The use may be interim.* Office uses (even light manufacturing or a shipping room as above) provide a viable interim (or even long-term) economic use and also contribute to street life. Even residences may be appropriate in some locations as an interim use until the neighborhood has grown enough to warrant more retail space.

Pasadena, CA

"Fill up those moats": the special problem of the shopping mall

The auto-oriented shopping mall and its progeny, the "power center" of big-box stores, dominate retail America. Is there any hope for them?

Yes, if one understands the Three Rules.

The astoundingly comical store above — when I first saw it I thought it a satire of the worst sort that could exist in an otherwise urbane environment — is unfortunately not a joke.

But the mall on the facing page — essentially no different than hundreds of malls across North America except more successful — is a striking example of the power of the Three Rules to transform. The city desired a pedestrian-oriented street. The setback had been heavily landscaped to block the view of the massive parking garage behind it; the result was creation of an "urban moat." But that planting area created an opportunity for urban backfill. The property owner eliminated the parking-lot buffer, an otherwise dull setback, and built outward to create a real streetfront of restaurants.

Bellevue, WA

A local newspaper recounted a talk by a representative of the property owner:

But perhaps the most telling indicator of the restaurant row's success was a photo [that] showed several pedestrians walking down a sidewalk outside the project. In the past, the executive told the group, such a scene probably would have required staging for marketing purposes. But these were bona fide pedestrians. "We were so excited when we saw this photo," she said. *"We didn't have to pay these people."*

It's a humorous, plaintive, but overall very hopeful sign that we can change the bleakness of an auto-oriented street.

All this city needs now is on-street parking and it will start to feel like a *real* city.

Bellevue, WA

CHAPTER 4

GETTING AROUND

I t is a cliche that we Americans are a people on the move. Mobility is one of the central values of U.S. culture. The right to travel is built into our constitutional bedrock; the road movie is part of our film tradition. We like to journey, to see things. Some say that this desire for physical mobility is the result of decreasing social mobility. Others say that we are living out genetic directions given to us by our nomadic ancestors.

In any case, the fact is we love our cars. And our boats and trains and planes and bicycles. Indeed, many of our sports involve the sensations of being in motion: skiing, sailing, flying, riding horses, kayaking, running, even walking; and many particularly involve wheels: cycling, in-line skating, mountain biking, skateboarding, and, of course, driving. We love motion with simple animal joy.

It seems we love the journey as much as reaching the destination. Transportation is a pleasure as well as a need. The Sunday drive is not on the wane; it is an American legacy that spans the generations. Any transportation policy that does not take into account our cultural proclivity and pleasure in motion is doomed to fail.

Of course the ostensible reason to get around is to meet people, for either love or money.

A comfortable city will allow quick and safe transportation for people of all income levels to and from any point without noise, danger, and pollution, and without destroying city neighborhoods and rural landscapes. It will permit several modes of transportation to exist. By this standard, however, there are no comfortable cities in the U.S. A great challenge to creating an urban village is moving people and goods in and out of it.

If there is one planning dogma held by many, it is that there is a panacea for the transportation problems of creating cities of comfort — and it is rail. In fact the belief in rail approaches an article of faith. There are plans for multi-billion-dollar heavy and light rail systems. But these calls may be as much wishful thinking as anything; the effectiveness of these systems is increasingly under question.

That is not to say that rail transit might not have some very important role. Light rail systems in particular have enormous potential. Small spurs can be cut and fit into an existing urban fabric, prove themselves, and thus systems can grow incrementally.

But this book is not about the merits or demerits of any particular transportation technology. With a few exceptions, it is devoted to showing relatively small things that can be done in six months, a year, or five years from now. Bridging freeways to reconnect neighborhoods is probably the most complex item in this book and should be able to be done in five or so years — even what would appear simple takes time these days.

Effective planning for pedestrian-oriented cities recognizes that this frame of mind is at the root of American culture.

Cars have wrought great destruction to our cities. But, starting from our current context, there is nothing magic about mass transit either. The job of building a rail system can be botched. Its success will depend on careful detail work. If a planning authority can't do that now with streets — which seems the case — why will it be able to do it with rail? What will likely be ignored — as is typical with enormous capital projects of any kind — is the fine-grain finish work to make it comfortable. In fact the hot debate over rail vs. buses vs. cars vs. heavy rail vs. elevated monorail vs. light rail typically proceeds with little attention to how things are to be done.

I fear that such debates over the wisdom of building rail systems will take the place of truly discussing the built environment and deter us from dealing with the thousands of small things we can do now and in a few years to build better cities. We will plan to buy a fire truck while Rome burns.

Traffic calming

Along with contextualism in the design of buildings, the most significant new idea in city planning in the last thirty years is traffic calming.

Traffic calming is a set of street design techniques. It involves a variety of small modifications to street geometry and dimensions to accommodate the automobile and yet give the pedestrian psychological precedence.

These techniques assume — as Buckminster Fuller did — that we should reform the environment, not personal behavior. Rather than modifying human behavior, Fuller suggested that it is far easier to get people to act differently by redesigning their environment.

Traffic calming also recognizes that the car will not wither away. It is too popular and indeed too sensible to disappear. Here is an instrument that gives people personal autonomy over their own lives, their own daily to and fro. People struggle for freedom and the car is a very real means to use it. The car will not disappear without authoritarian rule.

But too many cars lead to uncomfortable cities. The person as driver overwhelms the very same person as walker. The real icon of America should be Janus, the god with two perspectives: one the driver, the other the walker. Some form of peaceful coexistence between our personas as driver and walker must be found.

Consider the annoying and dangerous phenomenon of speeding. Ninety years after the first speeding regulations, and who knows how many speeding tickets later, many of us still exceed the posted limits. We do it because the roads are designed to allow us to do so. There is a natural speed for any given road configuration. Many roads are marked 30 miles per hour and yet are designed to be driven comfortably at 55 m.p.h. because of sight lines, lane width, and shallow curves. Design will win out. More police will not. Redesign the roads to make better use of our natural inclination to drive as quickly — or as slowly — as the road design itself suggests.

Traffic calming seeks to find such design solutions. Its theme is to moderate vehicles' speed, give more physical space to the walker, and reclaim some of the walker's space. Its goal is not to make driving impossible but to slow it down within cities to a more human pace.

We illustrate with a variety of techniques the basic principle of changing driver behavior though design. But the subject is so new, so complex, and so uncharted that the reader is forewarned that this is only the start of the possibilities.

Traffic calming through design should not be read to mean that human behavior is of no importance. For example, driver education could be broadened to include respect for pedestrians and the reasons for traffic-calming design. Many drivers are frustrated by traffic-calming devices because they do not understand the reason behind them — i.e., traffic calming aims not to anger drivers but to calm them.

Nantucket, MA

Consider curbs

The basic tool of traffic calming is the placement of the curb. Walkers may cross it; drivers may not. It defines their respective realms.

A rural lane — and perhaps even a low-volume city street — does not need a curb because the amount of traffic is trifling. There are not enough vehicles to create a sense of threat to the walker.

But a city is defined by greater traffic, and the curb provides order; it is a physical barrier. To drive over the curb onto the sidewalk is uncomfortable for the driver, hard on the car, and an outrage to social niceties.

The curb — apparently an insignificant line — nevertheless has a large part in defining how we experience the city. Moving it one way or the other changes the relative size of the pedestrian/car realms and their consequent sense of power.

Seattle, WA
photo by Barbara Gray

"Bulb" the corner for more pedestrian space

The struggle for urban space between walker and driver turns on a detail: the placement of the curb.

Moving the curb out into the roadway creates a "curb bulb." It is a superior and more comfortable spot for the walker crossing the street. It widens the sidewalk. It reduces the distance pedestrians must cross and makes them more prominent and visible to drivers. It takes back road from the driver and gives it to the walker.

Though largely made of concrete, the urban environment is really very plastic. Reshaping the curb line has a large effect on our use of the street.

Seattle, WA
photo by Walker and Associates

Build streets on a grid

Why even mention such an obvious thing as the continuous street grid? Probably because the suburban systems of cul-de-sacs became the predominant pattern of platting after World War II and the grid is not the automatic solution in subdivision. It is now a choice; but it is a choice not often made because of simple economics. Platting raw land based upon a system of cul-de-sacs creates more lots and hence more profit than does a rectangular street grid.

To clarify further, it is not critical that the grid be rectangular, i.e., a literal ninety-degree grid. The important thing is that the streets be continuous and create continuous thoroughfares. What one wants to avoid are dead ends, which tend to concentrate traffic on arterials rather than diffuse it through a broader network.

Additionally, a grid system allows a complex hierarchy of streets: arterials, collectors, and feeders, each one with different amounts of traffic.

Dedicated bike paths are difficult to establish and can never hope to satisfy the demand for bike routes. Restriping the existing street space to create bike lanes provides a greater opportunity. But continuous side streets, for example, as part of a grid make an excellent path for cyclists. They already exist and are a less trafficked and continuous route from here to there. These low-traffic feeders can, with very little investment, serve as bicycle routes.

Make blocks short

The short block (less than 240 feet or so) is a traffic-calming device of the first order. Short blocks mean more intersections. More intersections mean more places where cars must stop, thus lowering average auto speed. Short blocks also create more opportunities for walkers to cross the street. The short block is more interesting for walkers. A journey seems quicker, livelier, and more eventful when punctuated by crossing streets.

There's an economic attraction to short blocks: more corners. From a real estate value perspective, the corner is the best place to be: it has frontage on two streets, hence more visibility. Its cornerness also provides greater flexibility for site planning, which is the very first and most important part of designing a building. The corner at the intersection of a city's most heavily traveled thoroughfares provides the greatest access and visibility; it is traditionally the very best place in a retail district, its central place, and is known in the trade as "the one hundred percent corner." It represents the highest possible value, and everything declines away from that spot.

The value of corners is recognized for dwellings, too, as a house on the corner has more light and air than a midblock site and is typically more valuable.

Obviously it's a bit late, in most cities, to form a street grid with short blocks; most of our cities were platted (divided up into streets, blocks, and lots) long ago. Furthermore, it is not very easy to cut a new street through an existing block; one needs to condemn and purchase private property. We live with the glories and the mistakes of our forebears. Yet we are still expanding into the suburbs, building edge cities, and that gives us a chance to plat with short blocks.

Adding streets may be problematic; however, eliminating a street is often a cinch. The streets are a commons, and the "tragedy of the commons" is that no one cares for it as their own. Owners of adjacent property may request that the public's interest in a street be relinquished. This vacation — what a smoothly soothing term — of street right-of-way is a neat and low-cost way to increase the size of an urban property, but often at high cost to the streetscape.

Vacations were an urban planning fad in the 1950s and 1960s, which saw the development of the superblock. Here, two or more blocks plus the adjacent right-of-way are combined into one building site. The practice contributes to a city scaled for cars and is a grave error, but it is still being carried out as large institutions covet "free" land in the public right-of-way and local governments lend their approval to that transfer.

CKVILLE
301-770-6900

Kentlands, MD

Use shortcuts to create a grid

One naturally thinks that a sidewalk must be next to a road. But why not build sidewalks without streets?

For example, there may be a good reason to develop a new plat with some cul-de-sacs, or it may be already built. Such a pattern prohibits through traffic and creates quiet dead-end streets.

But it also creates few side streets, and all the traffic is channeled to a few arterials. One side of a cul-de-sac doesn't connect with another one. The parent with a stroller, the jogger, the child on a bike, or even the casual perambulator must detour to a busy street to go just a block.

The solution is to connect two cul-de-sacs (or two long parallel streets, for that matter) with bike-throughs. These can be installed when the plat is designed, but since they take so little space they would be a relatively inexpensive element in retrofitting an existing plat as well.

Here is a practical comfort test for the design of a new plat: children should be able to visit friends, get to school, and run to the store without having to walk or ride on a busy arterial. Some jurisdictions now require that site plans for new multi-acre developments show walking-time contours to specific places, such as a transit stop.

The bike-through shown here goes through a block of houses and connects two streets. It is a way for children to travel with less danger from cars and it creates urban spaces where cars cannot go, shifting the psychological feel of a neighborhood by creating car-free spaces.

Vancouver, BC, Canada

But don't let drivers everywhere on the grid

Interrupt the grid every so often. Block some intersections so cars cannot pass. When the street grid is broken, the speedy and sometimes annoying flow of traffic through a neighborhood is disrupted. But adding a bollard (a post which prevents vehicles from enering an area) to a curb cut allows fire trucks and ambulances to move rapidly when needed.

Breaking the grid may appear to contradict the idea of building streets on a grid, and to some degree it does. But both patterns should exist. We start with the presumption of continuous routing — i.e., the grid — and then vary it with devices for traffic calming and visual diversity. The resolution is balance, and viewing streets as a system.

CLOSE THE STREET

CARS CAN PASS IN AN EMERGENCY

Vancouver, BC, Canada
photo by Christopher K. Leman

And let cars and people mix

After all the emphasis these days on pedestrian-friendly streets it may seem coun-terintuitive to suggest that cars and people should mix. Wouldn't it be more civil and humane to create a place just for walkers? Take a busy commercial street, ban the cars, and leave it for people afoot. Such was the noble impulse behind the pedestrian mall. But it doesn't always work.

It isn't real, for one thing, and it's not something you can do many places. It's really inconvenient, and while it may be wonderful in theory, comfortable cities are built in practice. Behind the pedestrian-only mall is a theme-park vision of a city, something fascinating and quaint and worthy of a visit, but not something one might use every day. The reality is that we have personal vehicles. The task is not to ban them (impossible) but to calm them (readily done). Like the Colt .45 of the frontier, traffic calming is the equalizer of the auto age.

Mixing cars and pedestrians:

- Increases the eyes on the street — some pedestrian malls look pretty lonely.
- Maintains or even increases on-street parking spaces.
- Is convenient, will be used, and thus creates sustainable places.

Traffic-calming structures can be casual

Public works departments have authority over what happens in the street right-of-way (sidewalk and roadbed). They have a legitimate responsibility for public safety and for assuring improvements in that space.

Queenstown, New Zealand

But sometimes their requirements are set so high that nothing gets done. Here we see a very informal traffic-calming device that appears to work well, certainly at the very least as an experiment to determine how particular traffic devices will work.

(Traffic calming must be seen as a systemic approach, and with literally thousands of discrete intersections and conditions in a city, there is need for empirical experimentation.)

Decrease the turning radius

The various codes of city planners and city engineers, with their standards and requirements, form a "genetic code," a set of instructions to direct future growth.

These infinitesimal elements of a city's street engineering code have a large influence on our behavior as drivers and pedestrians. One key code standard is the "turning radius" of the curb at intersections.

This turning radius is determined by the placement of the curb and is the size of the circle that will fit in the corner. The smaller the circle's radius, the sharper the turn. The sharper the turn, the slower one must drive.

Typically, in a residential subdivision, the standard will be twenty-five feet. But by reducing this radius to fifteen feet, the engineer still allows free auto movement but signals to the driver that a slower speed is appropriate.

In addition, the narrower curve places the pedestrian closer to the goal: the other side of the street.

Seattle, WA

Slow traffic with circles

The traffic circle is simply a curb placed in the middle of an intersection — a deliberate obstruction in a stream of traffic, which forces drivers to slow down. It creates a quieter, calmer, and more "residential" environment.

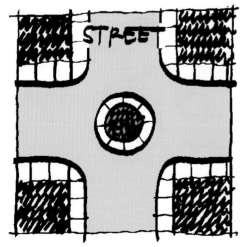

Once again, there are no silver bullets that solve all problems. The traffic circle is not manna. Some drivers loathe them and will change their route to avoid them, which may serve to decrease traffic on one block, only to divert it to another, increasing traffic there.

Use traffic circles only as part of a systems approach to neighborhood traffic. Their surface is a good place for neighborhood decoration.

Vancouver, BC, Canada

Consider roundabouts

Roundabouts are grown-up traffic circles. Their purpose is not so much to slow down traffic but to allow movement through intersections without having to stop. They are quite common in parts of Europe and are starting to be used in the United States.

The most frustrating aspect of urban traffic is not so much its overall speed but its stop-and-go nature. A slow but steady pace would achieve the same overall time from origin to destination but without the mental aggravation of continual acceleration, braking, stopping, and then accelerating again.

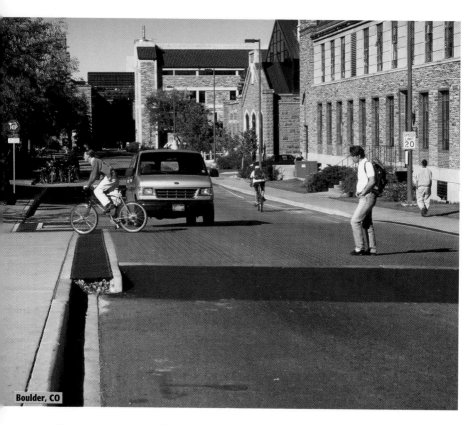

Boulder, CO

Raise the crosswalk

Let the pedestrian cross without stepping down onto the street bed. Raise the pedestrian crossing so that it is level with the sidewalk.

The extra six inches of height makes the walker more visible to drivers, particularly if one uses a pavement of contrasting texture and color. The change of grade is also a long-wave speed hump, which forces the driver to slow down to avoid an unpleasant bump.

Where entire intersections are raised so that traffic going in both directions will slow down, these intersections are known as "sleeping policemen" because of their ongoing deterrence effect.

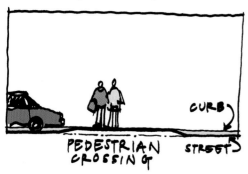

Seattle, WA

Curve roads to narrow sight lines

Traffic engineers are taught to hate curves in roads. Here is inertia, the most basic law of physics, manifesting itself. The path of least resistance is the path one is already upon; the curve is a detour and takes extra force to negotiate. A body at rest remains at rest; a body in motion remains in motion. The engineers want to let the car act like a stone in outer space, continuing on its path without diversion.

Curves slow down cars. Curves cause drivers to use their brakes. As the traffic engineer sees it, curves are to be straightened at any chance so that the traffic may flow more smoothly and hence more rapidly.

It is for precisely that reason that we should let the road curve. It makes drivers use their brakes. *It makes them slow down.*

It creates a slower and more tranquil environment when the car and the walker have to share the same space in cities. In fact, the new revolution of traffic calming will ask us to add curves in some situations.

Nantucket, MA

Olympia, WA

Narrow the street

Some streets are wider than they need to be for the traffic on them now or in the future. The excess room in the roadway can be given over to pedestrians or plants. The narrower street will signal to the driver to slow down as well.

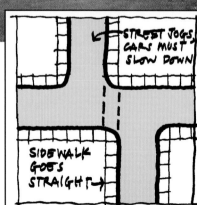

Jog to calm traffic

The street jogs, the car must slow; the sidewalk doesn't and the walker may proceed, giving symbolic precedence and greater ease to the walker. Whether this street pattern was planned or was an accident of platting has long been forgotten. But it works and is an example of a serendipitous detail.

Washington, DC

Consider vehicle size in street design

City streets are designed for the size and speed of the vehicles that are expected to drive upon them.

A city car need not be able to go 110 miles per hour. In fact, 30 m.p.h. is sufficient for a great number of trips. Twenty-five to 30 m.p.h. is a typical speed limit on most nonarterial streets. A vehicle much smaller and slower than our current cars — the golf cart, for example — would be adequate for many urban trips such as the quick run to the store. It would not be safe on the freeway, nor would it be comfortable on a long trip, nor could it carry a family of any size. But it does have a role. Our city streets would have a dramatically different feel if they were designed for and inhabited by the extremely small vehicle. Very small vehicles would also require much smaller parking spaces, thus, in effect, creating more parking slots for a given area or decreasing the size of required parking lots.

But to some degree, garbage and fire trucks determine the design characteristics of streets. That's reasonable. It would be mad to build a city that could not be protected from fire or in which garbage could not be easily removed. The public works departments of municipalities do a scrupulous job of ensuring that such vehicles can get around with ease.

But perhaps they do their job too well. Engineers may require street widths and turning radii larger than necessary and for vehicles bigger than needed. The result is more street and concrete for vehicles and less sidewalk and lawn for walkers, bikers, roller skaters, children at play, and plants.

Portland, OR

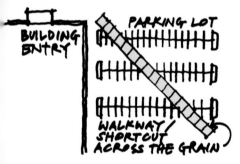

Allow shortcuts in parking lots

Like water flowing downhill, walkers find the shortest path; both manifest a similar law of conservation of energy. Shortcuts are a natural part of human behavior and should be accommodated, not thwarted.

What's annoying about many large parking lots is that their aisles often orient to an exterior wall of a building, but not with the main entrance.

Normally, the walker is urged by common sense to cut across the grain of the lot, but the cars are in the way and one ends up taking many small and annoying right-angle turns. Here, the urge to cut across the grain is acknowledged and welcomed. Planted like an allée in a French garden, this path cuts across the grain and provides a natural shortcut to the building entrance.

Here, designers oriented the convention center's main entrance to the street and relegated the parking lot to the side.

Seattle, WA

Change the paving material

The change in texture is a visual and visceral signal to both driver and pedestrian of the appropriate boundaries for each at that particular location. Indeed, pavement in a rougher texture is known as a rumble strip. But the texture should be smooth enough so that older people, bike riders, and people with disabilities are not deterred.

Imagine the highway as a boulevard

In the law, one may live or die depending on one's intention. Striking a person dead with an automobile may bring a death sentence if one intended the death; or, if the act was an accident, it may yield no more than a traffic ticket, if even that.

Our intention is also relevant when we think of our roads. We may think of the limited-access roadway as purely a means of getting from here to there. But if we intend the same transportation corridor as a parkway or boulevard it will have a very different feel. It becomes a more appealing road and provides a sensuous and comforting experience to the driver and the neighbor.

Washington, DC

Plant trees to slow traffic

A row of big trees along the road will cause drivers to slow down. The trees may not provide a physical impediment to speed, but they do have a real psychological effect by looming over the road and creating a hard and dangerous edge that protects the walker. They signal to the driver a place of repose, a place to linger and to glide rather than to rush.

Nantucket, MA

Nantucket, MA

Let commercial streets flow two ways

Ever since the 1950s, traffic engineers have sought to increase the "throughput" of traffic in a neighborhood by making two adjoining streets act as one. One street would be made all one-way in one direction. The adjoining street would be made all one-way in the opposite direction. Such a couplet would increase the number of cars able to flow through a neighborhood. This approach is good for cars but not for the neighborhood. The traffic engineers correctly realized that drivers tend to slow down when facing opposing lanes of traffic; the opposing lane creates a sense of friction and slower speeds. Thus if one's goal is to move as many cars as possible through a neighborhood, the couplet works well. But if the goal is to create comfortable shopping districts, make streets two-way.

Drivers tend to slow down when facing opposing lanes of traffic.

Here again is a detail of great importance to our lives that is so big it is virtually invisible.

Break up parking lots with trees

One of the reasons parking lots are so unpleasant is that they appear so big. An extraordinarily cheap and simple way to make a parking lot friendlier is to break down its perceived size by planting trees. Especially in lots with angle parking, there are generally leftover spaces where cars can't fit but a tree could grow.

Former first lady Lady Bird Johnson was right about the importance of beautification. If one were to do nothing to strip malls beyond landscaping them bountifully, it would transform these barren wastes into something quite comfortable.

Sidney, BC

Allow on-street parking to create a Main Street

There is a necessary and inevitable tension between the street as a conduit of vehicles *through* an area and the street as the *public space* of a neighborhood.

Many suburban areas yearn to leave behind their strip-mall origins and become real cities with a pedestrian orientation. They could do so, literally overnight, by allowing on-street parking (for at least the off-peak hours, evenings, and weekends). A simple sign that allows on-street parking can be the "tipping point" to create a main street.

A row of cars acts as a traffic-calming device — remember or imagine how unpleasant it is to sit/stand by a curb with cars driving even at only 25 or 30 miles per hour in the curb lane.

A row of cars at the curb acts as a buffer between the pedestrian on the sidewalk. It creates drag to slow cars. Drivers must reduce speed so as to be able to stop for unseen children, dogs, and car doors.

In an existing Three Rules neighborhood, merchants also benefit from the short-term parking and loading that on-street parking provides. What is good for small stores that use neighborhood parking is by and large good for the neighborhood.

Tokyo, Japan
photo by Hiromitsu Yajima

Seattle, WA

Park in commons

Neighborhood shopping districts — along with the local schools — are what give character and charm to a neighborhood and make it into more than an area. It is the relationship of building, parking lot, and sidewalk that determines the feel of a neighborhood shopping district. When merchants heard that suburban-style front-of-the store parking would be banished from Seattle's urban-village planning, they were alarmed. The traditional view of the postwar era has been that people will not walk and that the bare minimum distance between their car and the front door is the maximum they will tolerate.

Underground parking is quite expensive; rooftop parking is usually undesirable. A practical alternative to parking in the front yard is to park at the building's rear. But this has its own difficulties: either the customer is forced to walk around the block to get to the front door or the merchant must have two entrances, which may preclude the needed backroom and create an additional door to secure.

On two reasonable points, then — accessibility and security — the merchants argued for parking in front of the store.

Their problem is compounded if there is no alley for vehicle access to the rear of the site. Furthermore, many small shopping districts were platted before cars were pervasive, and at a smaller scale than we are accustomed to now. A typical lot may be forty to sixty feet wide, or even smaller, which leaves little room for a driveway leading to the rear of the property. Where, pray tell, does one put the parking if not in front?

One solution is to rely on the commons of on-street parking. But this well can run dry very quickly, even when augmented by angled or head-in parking. How, then, do we preserve and enhance neighborhood shopping? Merchants are quite right: customers need accessibility. But they can certainly walk one block from a public lot — they walk even farther at the regional mall.

So what about a neighborhood parking commons, a lot shared by many merchants in exchange for payment into a parking fund?

Here planners create what individual property owners are unable to do alone. Instead of required parking for each site, property owners pay into a common pool for a common parking lot. The streetwall is preserved, yet accessibility is assured.

But there are two issues.

The first is that an overly enthusiastic parking authority could build one massive and central parking structure instead of a series of small and scattered lots, which could be designed to fit in with the existing scale.

The other is that anti-car ideology will prevent us from taking incremental steps to improve things now.

Build with alleys: let cars use the servants' entrance

Something as simple as an alley is often ignored, but an alley is an elegant solution to getting the car onto the site without crossing over the sidewalk. Since there is no need for a curb cut on the street, there is also more space for on-street parking. Streets composed of houses and gardens and unbroken by cement and garages are more pleasant and economically valuable as well.

Klahanie, WA

Alleys are a holdover from an era when there were servants who entered through the servants' entrance. Alleys are particularly useful in commercial areas, allowing deliveries without interfering with pedestrians.

One developer (right) realized the value of the alley and worked it into his plan and advertising, which read, "Here's the very newest 'old' idea since *Leave It to Beaver*! We're giving you back your front yard because we put the garage in back — where it belongs."

Ironically, the municipal authorities insisted that the builder make the alley as wide as a street in order to accommodate fire trucks.

Bicycles

Two observations:

- Sixty-three percent of all automobile trips are less than two miles.
- On reasonably flat ground an average person in normal health can ride a bicycle 8 miles per hour.

So sixty-three percent of all automobile trips could be done by a bicycle in fifteen minutes or so.

Obviously that's only two-thirds of all auto trips, so bicycles are not a panacea for our transport problems. Certainly bikes are inconvenient in rain, in winter, in steep topography, and late at night.

That approach is part of the problem. It is easy to fall into the trap of thinking that all problems must have one big and glorious solution. We're always looking for the silver bullet and the home run that will solve all problems. Consider the urban transportation problem. Conventional thinking sees only costly answers such as superhighways and subways.

But such answers follow from a misstatement of the problem. There is no one transportation problem but a great number of smaller issues of mobility.

"Bikes won't solve the problem" is true if you are looking for one solution for all problems. Take into account the negatives of bike riding: winter, dark, cold, rain, steep hills.

Still, just suppose bicycles could be used to replace only five percent of all automobile trips. Certainly it's not the one hundred percent solution. But it's a gain. Five percent of a very big number is still a very big number. And what's wrong with a small gain?

But we don't have the patience to piece together the many small solutions that add up to solving big problems. We mock them and ask, as one Supreme Court justice recently did (in a land-use case involving a hardware store), "How many bathtubs can you carry on a bike?" In fact, as any homeowner or contractor knows, a very great number of trips for supplies are indeed for items small enough to fit in one's pocket — the washer for the bathtub faucet, for instance — much less a bike carry-bag.

Viewed in this context, an approach that might be appropriate for only sixty-three percent of automobile trips is worth a serious look.

But the main impediment to making bicycling a practical element of city life is riding safely among cars.

Separate dedicated paths are one solution, and herein lies an interesting debate in the bicycle community. Some bicycle advocates urge the construction of a system of bike-only paths throughout our cities. Others claim that because such a system would be a new and expensive circulation network, it would be cost-prohibitive and thus never be built. Furthermore, they point out that since bicycles are already a legitimate form of transportation, they should be given their due and the existing right-of-way should be redesigned to accommodate them.

Carry bikes on mass transit

One other issue for bikers is the "long haul" across the metropolis. Some people are reluctant to bike to work, or for pleasure, to a relatively distant destination out of fear that they will not be able to bike home comfortably due to bad weather or fatigue.

Partnering bikes with mass transit (buses, rail, monorail) makes sense. It gives the cyclist convenient access to the larger transportation grid.

The external bike rack shown here is simply one solution, and it may not be optimum. The bike must be attached to the rack with care by the rider, who may not know how to do it quickly, which will slow down the boarding process. The rack has limited capacity and exposes the bicycle to the full fury of weather and road grime.

Light rail, too (right), can accommodate bikes.

One key to realizing a social return on the huge investment in public transport is to ensure that it can link up with people in as many ways as possible.

Seattle, WA

Portland, OR

San Diego, CA

San Diego, CA

Provide bike storage

Another problem with bikes as an integral part of a transport system is storing the bicycle securely at the destination, or at the origin if one is linking to mass transit.

It takes only a short purposeful bike ride to bring home the importance of bike racks and to demonstrate how few they are: a small thing, but their scarcity is a real impediment to bike use.

A sophisticated urban transit system will also have facilities at park & ride lots and stations where bikes can be stored in safety, repaired, rented etc.

A bike rack can be simple, inexpensive, easy to install, even serendipitous. The one (left) was installed to define a sidewalk cafe. But it acts like a wall — for bicycles — without interfering with pedestrians. It is also useful as a footrest.

San Diego, CA

Aiken, SC
photo by June Murff

Let users control traffic signals

This cyclist (right) is activating the traffic signal so that she can safely cross a very busy arterial. Such a small detail — a signal-change button placed so that it is convenient for cyclists — is the kind of thing often ignored and lost in the battle over the big issues.

In a different but related context, above, the equestrians have a signal activator suitable for them.

Both cases show consideration for the user.

These little bits of infused intelligence scattered about our landscape are what's exciting about cities and what makes them work. The essence of city planning is to grapple with the larger systems while remembering the simple details that make all the difference in city life.

Vancouver, BC, Canada

Seattle, WA

Provide access for all through "universal design"

Mobility for people with physical disabilities has become an ongoing concern in design of all objects, large and small. As the North American population ages, this trend will surely increase.

But it is important to recognize that adaptations in architectural design can benefit everyone and make a comfortable city for all. Most adaptations for people with disabilities turn out to offer a high degree of convenience to people of all ages, sizes, and abilities. Using universal design at the outset reduces the need for adaptations and retrofits later on.

Seattle, WA

The exit gate above is wide enough for a wheelchair or scooter or stroller to negotiate, and less confining for able-bodied walkers as well. Almost all doors could be widened so.

Everyone loves to go to the beach. This ramp (left) allows people in wheelchairs and those who have trouble with steps to enjoy sitting by the water, too. They also make it easier for parents with strollers, older people with walkers, and skaters.

Seattle, WA
photo by Barbara Gray

Increase signal length/decrease wait time

Giving people time and attention shows respect, or lack of respect, as in the expression "not giving a person the time of day."

The timing of our traffic signals should give people precedence over cars. The typical signal is set to allow four feet per second of street crossing. That is to say, if the street is forty feet wide, then the light will be green for ten seconds. To permit more fragile populations — the elderly, those with disabilities, the very young — to cross with ease, set the signal at 3.5 feet or less per second of crossing time.

The character of one high desert city comes from its strikingly wide streets — nine lanes in many cases — a holdover from its pioneer days when a design constraint was the space needed by an ox team to turn full circle. But its walk signals are very short. Walk fairly quickly and before you are a third of the way across, the green WALK turns to red WAIT. Suddenly the pedestrian faces a phalanx of impatient vehicles.

Another detail to consider is the wait time for the pedestrian. The longer the pedestrian must wait to cross, the lower the respect shown. Long wait times — as long as three minutes — encourage pedestrians to violate the rules, putting everyone at risk. Making people wait is no different on the sidewalk than in the corridors of power.

But traffic signals can be adjusted. In an urban village the walker will have time to cross the street and without undue waiting.

Seattle, WA
"Meridian Archway" by Chuck Greening with Mare Kern and Robert Williamson

Build ramps with subtlety

So cleverly and gracefully was this ramp constructed that one might use it — with great pleasure — for several years before realizing that it was designed to comply with a law requiring universal access. Such understatement and discretion is part of making our social spaces accessible to all and making all people comfortable.

Alexandria, VA
photo by Elizabeth Kanny

Make busy sidewalks wider

The twelve-foot-wide sidewalk allows two couples to pass each other easily and with only minimal and unconscious maneuvering and no interruption of the conversation. But make the sidewalk wider yet if you want to accommodate public seating.

We design our street systems to allow free passage of automobiles in opposite directions. Should not the same consideration be given to walkers so that people walking in the opposite direction can pass without inconvenience?

Seattle, WA

Provide a midblock crossing

Some blocks are very long. Their very length encourages jaywalking: a bad thing, supposedly. Interestingly, there are planners who think that jaywalking should be the norm in cities and that such pedestrian use of the street is a sign of a healthy place where pedestrians have precedence over cars.

Nevertheless the wise traffic engineer will channel the urge to jaywalk—which is in its own way merely an attempt to make things more efficient — rather than attempt to deny it. The real problem is safety: how to signal to drivers where the walker has the right-of-way. Here, a change in paving and concrete posts with inset down-lights create prominence for a midblock crossing.

Alexandria, VA

Provide curb ramps

We make great strides in accommodating people in wheelchairs with this
simple ramp. There is also a benefit in
this simple detail — another example
of "Universal Design" — to older
people with walkers and parents with
strollers.

Make special consideration

As we grow older, we may not be able
to move as quickly or as easily as we
once did. Dedicated parking spaces
are polite and will benefit us all, in
good time.

CHAPTER 5

KNOWING WHERE YOU ARE

It is very disturbing to be lost; it is a nightmare. Accurate orientation, even if unconscious, gives us comfort, safety, and the sense of territoriality we need to take action in defense of our community.

Senator Bill Bradley's genius as a basketball player, wrote John McPhee, stemmed from his peripheral vision. It gave him an extraordinary sense of location on the basketball court. He could see a teammate ready to throw or an opponent ready to pounce out of the corner of his eye and beyond the range of most players. He had a split-second jump. He was always poised and comfortable because he knew what was going on around him.

So, too, it should be for all of us on the larger court of city life. The earth is a very big place, and the modern metropolis bombards us with information: roads, buildings, signs. When they all look the same — all too often true these days — it is easy to lose orientation, to become confused, lost, and isolated. Simple things can give us a sense of place and situation within the enormity of the city: street signs that can be seen even at night (or in the daytime if one is partially sighted), bulletin boards and interpretive signs, landmarks visible from many places, windows onto the visible workplace. Familiarity in a city breeds comfort.

Carmel, CA

We orient ourselves by listening, and we learn by observing. But the quickest test of knowledge, and the fastest way to gain an intimate understanding, is to teach someone else. Such articulation forces us to consider the subject very closely. When we are the teacher, the guide who is orienting others, we become more at home. *The Great Gatsby*'s narrator tells us how he had come to New York to seek his fortune and had taken a bungalow in a suburban "commuting town."

It was lonely for a day or so until one morning some man, more recently arrived than I, stopped me on the road.

"How do you get to West Egg village?" he asked helplessly.

I told him. And as I walked on I was no longer lonely. I was a guide, a pathfinder, an original settler. He had casually conferred on me the freedom of the neighborhood.

One of the most appealing things about a village — of any scale — is that it is small enough to be comprehensible. "Here is Main Street. Here is the grocery. Here is the school." One knows without special training. To make a comfortable city or an urban village, leave signs and clues that tell people where they are.

Vancouver, BC, Canada

Give people the time of day

Place clocks in public places. It is a simple convenience and represents the deeper social coordination given by our system of time measurement.

There is a tyranny of time: we meter out our days for dollars, the long nightfall of "no time" looms over our every day, and time is a gift we give to each other when we care.

But above all in a market economy, time is a useful tool to organize our lives. Having clocks readily visible, though not as useful now in the age of cheap watches and car radios, is still a small nicety, particularly at a bus stop.

Seattle, WA
"Sundial" by Chuck Greening and Kim Lazare

Tell time by the sun

This sundial built into the ground reminds us that time is rooted in the natural cycles of the earth and sun. It was not invented by Swatch®. The ancients could make amazing predictions with shadows. Here, one is invited to tell the time of day by using one's own body as an indicator.

Use foreign tongues

It's a gracious and courteous gesture to adjust one's language to the eyes and ears of visitors. For travelers in a distant land, a little bit of their own tongue is reassuring. It is essential for any city claiming to be international.

Seattle, WA

Amplify traffic lights

People who can't see well still need to get around. These traffic lights give them a signal they can hear to tell them when it's safe to cross the street. The small speakers (circled above the light) "chirp" when it's clear to walk in the north-south direction and "cuckoo" when it's "green" east-west.

This convention reflects an international standard so that vision-impaired people feel comfortable while traveling. Further subtleties are available such as user activation.

Sidney, BC, Canada

Seattle, WA

Reveal destruction and redemption

Many people grow up thinking that the natural cycle of the year starts with football and ends with baseball. It is important that from the earliest possible age people get a sense of other natural cycles, such as the upstream migration of the salmon.

Early in this century, the Army Corps of Engineers built a set of locks to connect the salt water of Puget Sound to the fresh water of Lake Washington. Salmon, however, are not boats and need the stimulation of rushing water to find their way upstream to their spawning beds. The locks disrupted their passage. To restore the run, the Corps built a fish ladder, an artificial switchback of swiftly running water alongside the locks.

Here, at a window below the water's surface, a mother and child observe the salmon as they migrate from salt water to fresh water.

Without human agency, this fascinating viewpoint would not need to exist.

Burlingame, CA

Enhance neighborhood identity with street trees

Repeat the same species of tree on one block, then a different species on a different block. Or perhaps different trees for longer street lengths or even a whole neighborhood. Naturally, issues of monoculture and species diversity and resistance to spread of disease arise when one wants to plant a large area with one species. But certainly a block might not be too big an area for one type.

The pattern of planting will be evident, enhance a sense of place, and give veracity to neighborhood names such as Magnolia and Madrona. Flowering trees provide an unfolding progression through the seasons to tie the city together.

Seattle, WA

Make signs speak directly

We live in the midst of an ongoing public conversation; it consists of the written signs we use to give directions and explanation. A sign that merely said "Be Careful" would not be nearly as effective as this one, placed by a concerned neighboring restaurant. Traffic engineers know that in some situations a unique and nonstandard sign catches the driver's attention and speaks more forcefully.

near Portland, OR
photo by Agri-Business Council of Oregon

Identify the crop

These days it is mainly farmers who can tell what crop is growing. Identifying those green tufts in the field is virtually an unknown skill for the vast majority who live in the city and suburbs. So signs that tell the names of the crops are useful.

Contrary to Gertrude Stein, there is always a there, there. But few people can see it. The delight of travel with a geographer (or other expert in landscape) is that each turn of the road and roll of the hill brings new objects onstage for observation, identification, and discussion.

Identify the plants

Naturopathic medicine is based on principles of self-healing and uses derived from ancient medicinal plants. On a south-facing slope next to the sidewalk, a college of naturopathic medicine grows many of them in order to educate its students.

To the casual passerby this garden is a jumble of unusual plants. The key map shows which plant is where and reaches out to the neighborhood so that it, too, understands the college's approach to health.

There were many unusual plants adjacent to my office door, which is somewhat unusual for commercial landscaping. People stopped to ask me their names and I was always stumped. So I had some signs made up to identify them.

Seattle, WA

KATSURA
Cercidiphyllum japonicum

Katsura is a small to medium-sized tree native to Japan. Its leaves are heartshaped like the redbud but arranged opposite instead of alternately. Fall colors range from yellow to smoky pink. A good urban tree.

HORTICULTURAL CONSULTANT DAPHNE LEWIS
SIGNS COURTESY OF CITY COMFORTS

Seattle, WA

Los Angeles, CA

Let individuals and groups take "ownership"

The tragedy of the commons is caused by no one caring about the sustainability of a community resource because no one owns it and so each person has a perverse stake in taking as much as possible quickly as possible. But even individuals can take symbolic ownership of a public space and should be encouraged to do so.

London, England

London, England

Warn pedestrians

Orientation even in what would seem to be the most trivial matters can sometimes be a life-and-death matter.

Portland, OR

Create gateways for neighborhoods

The medieval gate around the walled city was a way to create security. In the modern city there is pressure on civic authorities to turn public streets into private ones by allowing neighbors to install real, lockable gates; such an approach signals defeat in our effort to create civility.

But the gateway as a mere announcement can also create neighborhood spirit — and security — even if it is merely a token frame. Organized police work best with people who feel ownership of their neighborhood; small symbols, like an entry arch to a neighborhood, help to create that feeling. Suburban home-builders have known this for years and often put decorative pillars and columns at the entrance to their tracts. Should not city planners also be concerned with the sense of identity in neighborhoods?

Portland, OR

Let pedestrians see from bridges

Bridges provide a marvelous opportunity to see and comprehend the landscape without even going to any place special. Bridges are already at a special place: where a road crosses a river or a deep ravine. Such places have historic importance; cities grew up around them because they were places where goods had to be taken off the donkey and loaded on the boat, and vice versa. The control of bridges has been of great importance in both war and trade. Bridges — often difficult to build — are prizes and a focal point in any city.

While still very important, in the auto age they have become narrower in focus. Our single-mindedness about moving cars has led to bridges without places for cyclists or walkers, much less mere sightseers. But bridges can provide a delightful place to stop and ponder that which lies below and beyond.

Detail the grade

In the course of working with archi-tects the issue of grades and steepness will appear. The architect might try to explain why a driveway can't be built from this side of the lot or why steps — rather than a ramp — are needed in another situation. The explanation always refers to degrees or percent of slope. One might won-der what that feels like in real-world terms. One accepts their opinion that a ramp with more than a, say, eigh-teen percent grade is marginal, but one might want to experience it for oneself. Where could one go to sense steepness? The response is always a shrug, even though a fine school of architecture is only twelve short blocks away. Certainly design students need a visceral understanding of the difference between ten and eighteen percent (or is it degrees?). One might expect the university neighborhood to be scattered with marks on the pavement indicating different slopes so that the students could go out and experience the difference in grades before taking exams.

San Francisco, CA

1. **H**uman food can be harmful to birds.
2. **B**ird droppings throughout the park are unsafe, unsanitary, and unsightly.
3. **D**ense bird populations increase their chance of contracting disease and parasites and may attract rats and other nuisance animals.
4. **B**ird droppings add nutrients to the lake that increase algae growth which can cause lake decay and kill fish.
5. **P**arasites on waterfowl can cause "swimmers itch."
6. **W**aterfowl eat the grass that is needed for ground cover and erosion control.

Thank you for your assistance.
Call (206) 684-7053

Seattle, WA   Seattle Department of Parks and Recreation

Explain the rule

Many of us, libertarians at heart, only reluctantly admit that in order to maintain civic order and ecological balance, there are times when it is necessary to tell people what not to do. But rules are most effective if the reason why is also explained. In this sign, children and parents understand why we must curtail the natural and sometimes charitable impulse to feed the animals.

Mukilteo, WA

Elucidate temporary and small-scale relationships

This sign helps deal with the following and annoying dilemma: being in a queue with no knowledge of how long the wait will be.

If we go to the head of the line to investigate, we are concerned about dirty looks for being considered a line jumper. But then, if the wait turns out to be bearable, and we go back to join it, we may end up farther back in line because of new people who have joined the queue in our absence.

Identify clean places to eat

A weak link in the regulatory process, as it applies to retail locations, is that the typical consumer is never informed about the status of the places that he or she frequents. In San Diego, restaurants are required to post a sign indicating how well they comply with the health code. Such a procedure gives the consumer a means to judge the safety of an establishment.

San Diego, CA

New Zealand

New Zealand

Identify local activities

There are many advantages to the global village, but the lack of local identity that sometimes ensues is not one of them. So bring out what is unique in your locality.

near Salem, OR

Reveal the global framework

Latitude and longitude were one of the earliest methods by which we organized our world. But real as this measure may be, its scale is so vast as to be quite incomprehensible (blue-water sailors aside). An occasional reminder about where we are in this enormous global framework might be educational as well as amusing.

Salt Lake City, UT

Explain large-scale geologic relationships

Geology too is so big and complex that it is difficult to grasp. In much of the temperate zones, key elements are hidden under vegetation. So show geologic phenomena when possible.

Orient with music

Parking garages are typically confusing and disorienting. There is no outside light or view; there are no interior visual cues. All the cars and floors look the same. It is easy to forget the location of the car.

In this building the management created a musical theme — each floor a different city with characteristic music — to help people remember where they parked.

Explain signal synchronization

For greater efficiency, traffic lights down the length of an avenue may often be set to turn green in sequence, so that drivers may maintain a steady and even speed. It would be helpful to drivers and more efficient overall if they were explicitly alerted to the appropriate pace. There's nothing as foolish as hiding a useful system from its target users.

It should be noted that these systems are generally hostile to creating a pedestrian-oriented neighborhood because they are designed to simply speed traffic through and not much more. But such traffic measures will be with us for a while, so they should at least be done well.

Seattle, WA

Build bulletin boards

An urban village will surely include bulletin boards. Bulletin boards are cheap neighborhood mass media, efficient for the cost, and fun. They are a communications medium just as surely as is a television station except that they are a two-way system.

One can measure the health and vivacity of any type of community (town, neighborhood, or organization) by looking at its bulletin board. Likewise, a prospective employee can learn much by perusing a company's bulletin boards.

Some condominium associations and supermarkets do not allow bulletin boards because they are "too messy." That's a sad mistake. Community starts with communications. It's a sign of organizational bleakness if there is nothing but official notices. It's a bad sign, too, when there are private notices but they have been retyped by the management or placed onto standard forms. Even worse are those bulletin boards enclosed within locked glass doors.

Nantucket, MA

EVELENE AND GEORGE
BULLOCK

INVITE YOU TO
'SIT AND STAY'

Seattle, WA

Encourage people to leave their mark

They really don't need much encouragement, only an outlet. And it works out for the common good. As people grow older and more able to be philanthropic, their urge to be remembered in their old age and after their death becomes more compelling.

This urge for immortality is an ancient one; the Lascaux cave drawings are not diminished by describing them as a very brilliant piece of graffiti left behind so that the future would remember the artists and their skill.

No less than great museums, the Seattle parks department has recognized this very natural and human urge and capitalizes on it. It has a gift program that specifies objects, locations, costs, and so on.

The couple who gave this park bench are now even more rooted in their city's history.

Olympia, WA

Identify watersheds

After a landscape has been utterly transformed by urbanization, it's difficult to remember what was there before, what still underlies the concrete. It is astonishing to come across a construction site in the middle of a city — especially the central business district with its towers — and see that dirt — real dirt — is still underneath the concrete. It is very easy to forget that at one time — not very long ago — the entire world was wilderness and a road was a rare blessing. (One of the benefits of wilderness travel is that it reminds us why we have chosen the path of civilization.)

Likewise with watersheds: even though the stream may be long buried under streets and sidewalks, and running through culverts and storm sewers, it still exists, and so does its drainage basin. These signs remind us that no matter how much concrete has been poured, earth abides.

Olympia, WA

Remind people where the water goes

Out of sight, out of mind. That's a good explanation for why people will dump things like used motor oil down the drain when they wouldn't consider dumping it into their own swimming pool.

This stencil reminds people that the black hole of the sewer is really just an entryway to another world: our lakes, rivers, and oceans. It gives a practical message, reminds them of the law, and also communicates that some individual person — not distant "government" — cares about the fish.

Rancho Mirage, CA

Put maps on sidewalks

Any detail that helps us know where we are makes a city more comfortable.

These sidewalk maps help residents and visitors to get around without getting lost. It would be logical and obvious to put a map inside in every park and bus shelter. In the coming digital era, we should expect interactive maps. How helpful it would be to know the best route to such and such address or the location of the nearest Thai restaurant.

Paris, France

DEVELOPMENT APPLICATION
NUMBER 213720 1012 BROUGHTON STREET

TED MURRAY ARCHITECT
HAS APPLIED TO THE CITY OF VANCOUVER
FOR PERMISSION TO CONSTRUCT A THREE-
STOREY-PLUS-ONE-LEVEL OF UNDERGROUND
PARKING, MULTIPLE DWELLING BUILDING ON THIS
SITE CONTAINING:
     EIGHT (8) DWELLING UNITS
     EIGHT (8) UNDERGROUND PARKING STALLS

...ED FROM: ZONING ENQUIRES COUNTER
2ND FLOOR, EAST WING, CITY HALL

Vancouver, BC, Canada

Qui fait quoi ?

Concessionaire:

SOGEPARC

Architecte: HERVÉ AUGÉ
            PIERRE LEGOUX
            PHILIPPE MAXIN

Entreprise Générale:

CITRA   Coordinateur: MAIRE DE PARIS
                             Direction de la Voirie
Paris, France

2829 ASH STREET
HARD HAT AREA
WORKING HOURS
MON-FRI   7:30-8:00
SAT   10:00-8:00
CLOSED SUN. & HOLIDAY
STRICTLY ENFORCED
Seattle, WA

Leave no black holes of information where rumor and discord may flourish

No one likes surprises, especially if the surprise may be an unpleasant one. Most people consider anything new in their neighborhood to be unpleasant. It is wise public policy that proposed development should be announced and comment from neighbors solicited. Naming the architect and developer will add accountability. (The unwise part is that permits may sometimes be issued by the pound: one weighs the letters for and those against, and the permit is issued to the greatest weight and, mixing senses, the highest decibels.)

Developers need not look at these signs in only a negative light. Use them — within the guidelines, of course — in order to sell the project. The sign may be a sales tool, as well as public notice to the neighborhood.

The standard white board from Vancouver is, by force of Pavlovian conditioning, a more forceful announcement and seems to call forth action just as the red cloth animates the raging bull. Of course, with the architect's name on it, at least people knew who to call.

Communication during construction is also a good idea. People are genuinely interested in knowing what's going on. A sign may give people an understanding of their environment and a stronger sense of connection to it. Sometimes people need to know who to contact to complain; sometimes the sign can express the sheer fascination with and vicarious joy of building. One sign explains the rules on working hours. Yet another one, from Paris, shows that concern for the built environment is a global phenomenon and answer "Who does what?"

Seattle, WA

Divulge transit schedules

One of the more frustrating aspects of riding public transit is never being sure if one is early or late for the bus or even if the bus is running that day at all. I remember as a child waiting for several hours in cold weather for a bus that wasn't even in service.

Of course the truly excellent system would have buses departing so often that a schedule would be unnecessary. But until that day (unlikely to happen soon), post schedules at every stop.

Vancouver, BC, Canada

Allow workplaces to be seen

The world has become so complex that we easily lose touch with how it operates. This was not always so. In a simpler time, the commercial and industrial processes happened at a smaller and more accessible scale. One could see an economy at work. That is rare now, which is sad because understanding the basic processes of our world helps us understand our own position in it.

One of the negative effects of urbanization and factory production is that people have little understanding that somebody, somewhere, actually made the objects we see around us. Children especially should be able to see the way things are put together. The holistic viewpoint needed by the citizens of the future can be encouraged by exposing people to whole processes.

Further, there are few things more pleasing than to watch other people work, especially when the worker is skilled and the work is intriguing and involving. But few places allow close observation of other people as they shape the world.

The glassblowing shop in the photo above allows the visitor to see the creation of a glass object from raw material to finished product.

Seattle, WA

Explain unusual equipment

The fishing fleet moors here and repairs its nets and gear in full view. The port provides attractive signs that explain different aspects of commercial fishing. The docks themselves are open to the public to walk on. At first, when the design was unveiled, the fishermen were concerned that the lack of a fence would lead to accidents. But that has not been so. A certain common sense keeps people out of the way.

CHAPTER 6

FEELING SAFE

Human communications flourish only in safety. A prerequisite for meeting people or getting to know them better is feeling safe, secure, and unthreatened. Safety is at the root of city politics. Humans initially came together in settlements for increased security from wild animals, flood, famine, and enemies. When the chips are down, there is safety in numbers.

Of course, very large cities with great populations and high levels of anonymity have had crime problems for thousands of years. But now, greater mobility gives us the choice to add distance to our protective mechanisms: to move to ever more dispersed suburbs because cities make us uneasy — except in our locked cars. (And even cars are not safe havens, as carjacking shows.) So part of the question of city design — and suburb design, for that matter — must be "What patterns allow us to feel safe?" Without trying to explain the causes of crime, can design contribute to safety?

The first principle of security in any situation is surveillance. The basic technique of urban security is natural surveillance and human presence. And this should be no surprise. Intelligence is the first need for the army at war and the pedestrian on the street. Consider the function of the night watchman or the surveillance camera: to deter wrongdoers simply because they know they will be observed, and observation precedes arrest. But surveillance in our context does not mean formal watching but the casual observation that comes naturally, for example, when one is sitting on the porch after dinner.

The second principle is territoriality: people must view the public space as their own and thus take some responsibility for it. They must not only be able to see trouble as it develops, but they must also be willing to act and to intervene — if only to telephone the police.

What these principles mean in architecture is the creation of spaces where people are present and can observe each other in a form of mutual protection and where they have enough sense of ownership of the street that they will intervene in some way when trouble appears.

Jane Jacobs spoke of "eyes on the street," the presence of other human beings who care.

Tokyo, Japan
photo by Hiromitsu Yajima

Scatter police

"The cops are never around when you need them." So goes the old saw. One solution is to scatter small police stations, sized for one or two officers, about the city. If a vendor sells espresso nearby — a natural gathering and gossiping spot — so much the better.

Seattle, WA
photo by Barbara Gray

Put cops on bikes

Silent, fast, and physically fit from hours of riding each day, the cop on a bike is a formidable opponent for a scoundrel. Such an officer is also accessible and puts a friendlier face on authority, which is important. The police are only the tip of our security system and, like fish, rely on the water they swim through, the general population, for support.

Seattle, WA

Open the storefront to the street

How do you make the street an interesting place where people will linger? Every shopping-center owner knows that you have to slow down customers' pace and let them be drawn in by the merchandise. The same rule applies to the street.

People are a cautious lot. We enter through the door of a strange store with some element of timidity under the watchful eye of a strange shopkeeper. The wise merchant will make such an entrance as easy and inviting as possible. The shop with a fully opened and permeable front allows a delicate, slow, and uncommitted entrance. You stop to look at the plants on the street, then your eye is caught by an item farther back. "What's that thing in there?" And soon, without a decision, you're inside the shop. The permeable storefront is inviting and thus good merchandising.

No door or windows at all creates immediate opportunity for the shopper to enter and enables the shopkeeper to constantly and naturally observe the street.

Seattle, WA

Boulder, CO

Use interesting shopfronts to engage walkers

Interesting sidewalks are busy. Busy sidewalks are safer.

There is a beachfront on the island of Maui that could be one of the great promenades of the world: Kihei. It stretches for five or six miles along a grand bay. A two-lane road runs along its entire length. Much of the beach is public park. The land upland from the road is devoted to business. Between the glorious weather and the vigor of a long stroll, this indeed could be a memorable walk, the kind of stroll that by itself could draw one from a distant continent: a safe, dry, warm, and interesting walk, with many shops and stores to browse and amuse and keep the street alive and safe.

Alas: the many shops and stores are built in the strip-mall model, with the parking lot between the street and the stores. The walk along the road is boring, with no shop windows to peer into and only the hoods of slumbering automobiles to look at. We could see some mildly interesting shops across the parking lots. We wondered what they sold. But we did not walk over to look. Crossing the barren plain of parking-lot asphalt had no appeal. In fact, it was positively repelling. So we demurred, and the merchants lost sales. The parking lot was a barrier to profit.

Get close to the customer: build to the sidewalk and create interesting storefronts to give people something to look at as they walk.

Seattle, WA

Allow street vendors

Some cities have a policy of allowing street vendors to locate where they wish, subject only to veto of the adjacent merchant or property owner. The result is a node of activity. One espresso entrepreneur saw a space under a marquee, an empty niche. With espresso cart, tables, and chairs, it is now a place to relax from shopping. It promotes human contact by providing a quiet eddy to schmooze, out of the rushing torrent of downtown commerce. More eyes on the street also create safety.

Kentlands, MD

"Could you keep an eye on things?"

Again, a principle of such simplicity that it took Jane Jacobs's enormous insight to see it. But it is an insight that applies to residential areas as much as to shopping districts: "eyes on the street" promote safety. The price of liberty is continual surveillance. The old rule of the sea — "One hand for yourself, one hand for the ship" — applies on shore: "One eye for yourself, one eye for the neighborhood."

Place the entrance to a residence so that the visitor knows where to enter and neighbors can see what's going on. The Block Watch program of many neighborhoods is a way we formalize a practice that used to be a natural part of neighborhood life when neighbors actually knew each other.

"Eyes on the street" provide security. Thugs know this and, as you may notice, avoid breaking into homes while neighbors watch. But hide the door and you give them an opportunity for crime. It is the continual and casual surveillance of the street outside by the people inside that provides security.

Washington, DC

Make the main entrance visible

It's an aid to security if neighbors can see the front door. Well, it may not apply to this house as much as to most, since the folks who live here have full-time eyes on the street at every possible turn. But the principle is the same. The official police can't do everything, and they can't do much at all without good information. So the eyes and ears of the rest of us are essential to deter crime.

Further, it's perplexing and annoying to desire to enter a building and not know where to go. It means extra walking and backtracking and, if at night or in a less frequented area, it creates feelings of insecurity. It's a rude way to treat a guest. There is enough natural perplexity in the world. We don't need architects to give us ambiguous clues that lead us hither and yon before we can find an open door.

So make the front door obvious and start signaling its location at the sidewalk.

Sea-Tac Airport, WA

Open stairways to visibility

Extend the principle of visibility to the interior of a building. Stairwells, like parking garages, are notoriously creepy places. Most architects view them as a mere necessity of code compliance and pay them no attention. They tuck them out of sight and far from the main entrance. This stairway is located immediately adjacent to the elevator core and allows the casual passerby to observe activity in the stairwell, making it a safer place.

From an energy and building-maintenance perspective, stairways in smaller buildings can be used as a real means of mobility, not just a code necessity, by placing them at the main entrance.

CHAPTER 7

CHILDREN IN THE CITY

My city has the progressive policy of broadcasting its city council deliberations on a city-owned cable-TV station. One day the council was talking about children and the city.

It was a very interesting discussion about family composition and its relation to zoning rules and dwelling size. Like many American cities, my town is concerned about middle-class flight; this is understood to mean families moving out of the city to the suburbs. The council was pondering what, if anything, to do about this phenomenon. Some people were arguing for urban housing that would accommodate children: child-compatible housing. Others wanted to put more of an emphasis on revitalizing the school system.

The concern about families with children leaving Seattle was fascinating and intelligent. But I had a moment of concern — a moment of black humor — that others might misinterpret the council and see them at the top of a slippery slope: a politically correct city council discussing family composition. Might someone fear a notion — lurking in deep background — that along with numerical goals for such things as water quality, job growth, and traffic congestion there might also be a goal for the number of children in the city? For once you have decided that the city should be a place for children, wouldn't one

Queenstown, New Zealand

obvious way to ensure that your policies are working be to urge people to have children? But the council never even got close to such foolishness.

Their question was not whether or not children live in the city per se. The council was concerned that the city should be a hospitable environment for children. Children are like the canaries in a coal mine: an indicator species of urban health. Children are small and vulnerable and need to be protected. If a city lacks children, it is because parents have assessed the environment and have decided, one family after another over the privacy of the dining room table, to remove to a safer place. But where parents won't raise children, we might all hesitate to live, for such a place presents an environment uncomfortable, noisy, and dangerous.

Berkeley, CA
photo by Penny Niland

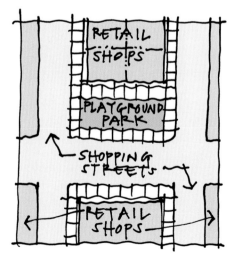

Place playgrounds in shopping districts

Combine adult seating with play-grounds in business districts. These places may be small. Place them at easily accessible locations, especially in shopping districts. This one is carved out of the public right-of-way on the edge of a busy street. (It serves to narrow the street to slow traffic as well.)

Children are more open about striking up acquaintances than are adults. So like puppies, children ease the way and make it natural and easy for adults to say hello.

Provide playgrounds in unlikely places

Children do not have the patience of adults; perhaps this defines them. Traveling with children can sometimes be trying because they get bored so easily. So provide little playgrounds even in the midst of intense development. Shown here is a playground in an intermodal (car/bus/ferry) terminal where tired parents can let their children catch up.

North Vancouver, BC, Canada

Provide simple toys

A paved surface can provide, so long as it's safe, a place for children (and even adults) to play.

Seattle, WA

Seattle, WA

Single-family neighborhoods are not exempt

Seats are appropriate even in neighborhoods of single-family dwellings. The bench shown is provided by generous residents on their own property.

Vancouver, BC, Canada

Build to child scale

Building spaces that are sized for children is a courtesy.

Build in baby-sitting

Children are more at ease when they have something to do. Most critically, children bother adults less when they feel at ease. Let them draw on walls that are primed for their touch, as they sit at chairs designed for their size.

Seattle, WA

Any one of several thousand McDonald's®

Provide playgrounds at restaurants

Mothers say that the places where a parent can lunch with friends while the children play safely are rare. It is a sad commentary on the state of city life — and a tribute to the acumen of McDonald's — that it is one of the few private institutions that provide such a comfort.

Parents and children need to be together without stumbling over and interfering with each other.

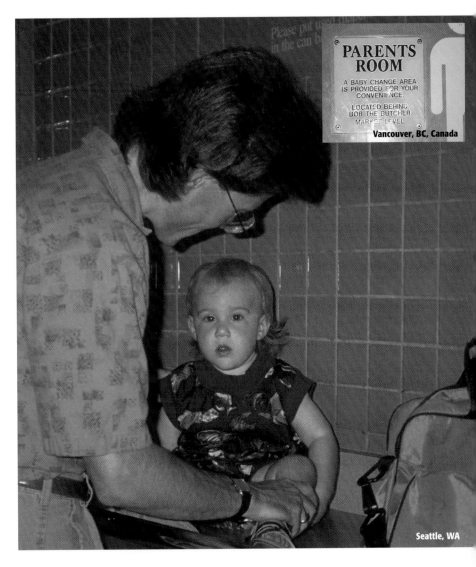

PARENTS ROOM

A BABY CHANGE AREA IS PROVIDED FOR YOUR CONVENIENCE.

LOCATED BEHIND BOB THE BUTCHER MARKET LEVEL.

Vancouver, BC, Canada

Seattle, WA

Let infants (and parents) travel in comfort

Diapers have to be changed, and not at the convenience of adults. So make it easy for parents with children to travel by providing appropriate counters in public rest rooms.

Society has a stake in having happy homes. Part of happiness is travel. Why should parents have to give up sightseeing when there are little ones? No reason at all if we make accommodation for parents.

People with disabilities are now considered in the design of buildings. Perhaps public accommodation should consider children as well.

CHAPTER 8

LITTLE NECESSITIES

Amyriad of small elements adds comfort to the city and makes it, well, comfortable. They are not large and glamorous but they make a difference indeed.

Much of our public discussion attends to abstract issues such as housing units per acre or levels of service (at intersections), but it is the tiny details that create an urban village.

Shelter the telephone

The cellular telephone has dramatically lessened the demand for public pay phones. But that doesn't mean you shouldn't shelter this little outpost on the information superhighway. Many phone booths are both inconvenient and uncomfortable to use because of exposure to noise and weather.

Public phones are a safety measure for the motorist stranded at night or the child lost during the day. Don't be stingy with phones (and keep 911 calls free).

Dunedin, NZ

Vancouver, BC, Canada

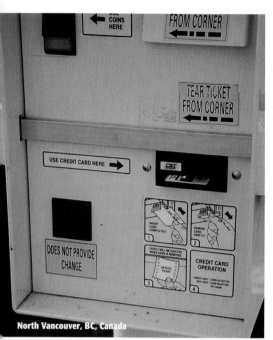

North Vancouver, BC, Canada

Pay parking with charge card

Who hasn't been stuck in a parking lot with not enough cash or bills too large?

Leave it to capitalists to make it easier for you to park your car, paying by charge card.

Seattle, WA

Provide ashtrays

A nasty habit indeed, but it's even nastier when the only place to extinguish the smoldering butt is on the sidewalk or between your thumb and forefinger. Yes, the public ashtray does raise the issue of benign tolerance for others' weaknesses versus encouragement of vice, but at least it dampens the problem of litter.

"Have a drink on us"

Nowadays, most of us take water for granted. But early human settlements grew up around rare wells and springs. Providing safe and cheap water through municipal waterworks was a massive social advance. In poor societies without in-home plumbing, the community well is still part of daily life and social progress is measured in something so invisible to us as safe drinking water.

Newer water fountains welcome people in wheelchairs with a cantilevered drinking spout, and welcome children with steps.

Seattle, WA

Cannon Beach, OR

Seattle, WA

Berlin, Germany
photo by Brian Livingston

Somewhere in Europe
photo by JC Decaux

Public toilets are a comfort

Public toilets are known as comfort stations for good reason. Even though everyone uses toilets, it's remarkable how few there are when needed — particularly clean ones. Public toilets are one of the first priorities for a comfortable city.

On a visit to New York my lunch companion announced that it was time to visit the loo. I made no motion and she reminded me that I was in the big city: "The experienced traveler should never pass up a clean bathroom." City comfort is made of small things.

The public toilet shown here is in Europe, where there are more than four thousand scattered about the public streets. It locks and cleans itself after every use. It can cost the local municipality nothing if — as is being done in San Francisco — advertising is allowed on kiosks or other street furniture.

Cannon Beach, OR

House the garbage can

Garbage cans are crucial to cleaner streets. They remind people, simply by their quiet, patient waiting, that the place for garbage is in the can and not on the sidewalk.

We should honor them by giving them attractive or notable shelter, particularly in locations where there are street vendors selling food.

Seattle, WA

Keep your head dry

So many of the amenities to make a city more pedestrian-friendly are pure common sense and solicitude.

Awnings are a friendly gesture; they extend a building's protection to the guest who passes along the sidewalk before it. Because awnings offer such hospitality, they draw pedestrian traffic to them and benefit the business of adjacent merchants.

Buckminster Fuller said that civilization, in its technology and tools, is simply a way of modulating and tuning — in and out — the elements: earth, air, fire, and water. Awnings are a humble but effective way to tune out a wet head.

Make it easy for pets to be polite

There is general agreement that pets are good for the mental health of their owners. This is particularly so in atomized urban areas where many people lack companions. Like babies, but even more so, pets are a vivid way for people to identify themselves and to recognize kindred spirits. Dogs are also an aid to safety by giving warning of prowlers.

But dogs, to some degree, create a problem. So . . .

Paris, France   London, England   Vancouver, BC, Canada

If you have these friends . . .   and you have these rules . . .   then get some of these tools.

Keep your feet dry

Create a narrow strip — sixteen inches or so — of concrete, brick, or any hard surface at the curb and extending into the planting strip to allow people getting out of a car to keep their feet dry.

One might think that such an insignificant detail as dry feet is too trivial to consider. But it is precisely such small details and courtesies that enrich life and make some cities a pleasure. Without such details, urban planning is simply the board game Monopoly for adults.

Seattle, WA

CHAPTER 9

FITTING IN

Economic growth involves a continuous reconstruction of society. Such rebuilding raises again and again the issue of ensuring that the new buildings do not war on the old, and thus, in the political sense, that new construction is politically sustainable.

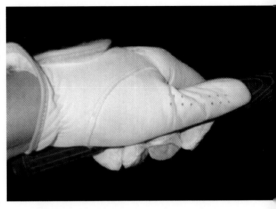

With buildings as with humans, there is a delicate line between attracting too much attention by overly dramatic self-presentation, and being a wallflower, ignored and unnoticed. Current thought is that it is best for a new building to fit in with the existing architectural context of its neighbors. The new building should in some way echo and mimic the materials, height, details, and behavioral patterns of its neighbors. This does not mean that the new building must exactly copy the old ones but simply that it should learn from and respond to the buildings that surround it. We call this approach "contextualism" and it does make a lot of sense. The key to creating a landscape where a new building fits in is clear communication to the builder through codes. But before that, the code writers must understand what is most important about any particular landscape.

Architects often talk about whether a building "talks" to its neighbors. What they mean is whether a building refers in its own shape and material to the shapes and materials of its neighbors. A lively conversation between buildings means that the buildings relate to each other. The color of one may be picked up and amplified by another or the roofline of another may be mimicked by yet a fourth. A group of musicians will do something similar in their playing. A horn may start with a cluster of notes, and the pattern will be repeated with variations by the other instruments.

Even the most elegant golf grip, too, is based on very simple elements.

Buildings are much like their human users. Conversation between buildings, as among humans, is a poignant sign of neighborliness. It is the height of rudeness — though all too often the expected norm in cities — for neighbors to speak not a word to each other for years on end. Buildings that do not talk to their neighbors are also rude.

Boston, MA

Successful contextual development also depends on a clear conversation between the government and builders. A zoning code that speaks clearly is a practical prerequisite to fitting in, because it is through the zoning code that the developer learns what is allowed and expected. It is through the zoning code that society speaks. Just as a great client stands behind a great architect, a great zoning code stands behind them both.

This great zoning code will be based on a close study of the environment that it seeks to protect. It will most often call for *unified diversity*. Not an oxymoron, this is an approach that allows variations, but only tight ones, from a clear theme. For example, the great townhouse neighborhoods of Manhattan and much of Paris and Boston are built to a very simple zoning code. The building can be only so tall; it can or must be built to the sidewalk; its entrance must be only in such a location; it must have so many windows; and so on.

One could write the zoning code for such areas on a postcard: short and simple. But out of these limits grow hospitable, attractive neighborhoods. The builder must pour his or her creativity into narrow confines: the detailing of windows, the color of the siding, the arrangement of the entry, etc. Like any other tight and limiting form — the haiku, the sonnet, the airplane — the creative and personalizing impulse must focus on only a limited set of variables.

For example, the photo on the left shows the delightful Newbury Street in Boston, made of buildings whose building envelope could be described on the back of a postcard, a small postcard at that.

The number of variables to be considered will depend on the tightness of the context and the degree of political desire that such context be preserved. For example, there are strict design guidelines for Nantucket Island, with even more specific parameters in the historic town of Nantucket. There are rules for all aspects of the building and its site, and many decisions are foreclosed. Flat roofs are simply not allowed. Roof pitch must be at least 4:12, or considerably steeper if neighboring structures have already set such a pattern. Nantucket is unusual. It has both a strong architectural context and the political will to preserve it.

There are a number of aspects that will determine whether a building fits in or not. For example:

• Site plan and orientation.
• Size, proportion, and scale.

These are generally dictates of the local land-use code, and there may not be much choice for the developer.

However, a developer may be given more latitude with other factors such as shape, roofline, windows and doors, exterior architectural elements, surface materials, trim and architectural details, and color.

Some codes are very restrictive and allow few choices; others are wide open and provide no sense of what is appropriate vocabulary.

In codes such as Nantucket's with tight constraints — like dress codes at a parochial school — the result tends to be (or at least should be) easy and predictable public administration. In neighborhoods governed by codes applying unified diversity, new buildings fit in without being slavishly identical, and may yet reflect the idiosyncrasies and preferences of owner and designer.

The only proviso with the fitting-in approach — and it is a major one — is that the existing context must be worth emulating, which is not often the case. Sometimes the neighborhood is in transition, such as when the zoning has been recently changed; or perhaps the existing built environment lacks charm. In either case there is little context worth saving or emulating. Here of course the contextual approach falls apart and the developer and neighborhood are free to face the enormous challenge of creating a new context.

But in general, the contextual approach provides a just challenge to the cutting-edge school of "rock-star architecture," which seeks the novel for its own sake, and for the sake of career advancement.

Seattle, WA

Look next door for context

The building on the left was brand-new in 1993 and made of modern materials: factory-made windows and an ersatz version of stucco. It fits in well because it follows the basic rules for commercial buildings: it is built right up to the sidewalk, it has retail on the ground floor, the retail has windows that face the sidewalk, and the main doors of the building face the street.

Of course, this building (to the left) was "lucky" because it had a strong and straightforward neighbor (to the right) to guide it.

Paris, France

Respond to modern preferences and fit in

Contextualism cannot reverse or deny the preferences of consumers. Modern users of both commercial and residential space have certain demands, and their needs must be met or there is no sale. It is possible for a new building to meet these demands. People like and have become accustomed to light-filled rooms. The light-colored building in the center of this photo responds to this modern demand and yet fits in with its older neighbors.

Close observation reveals that there is a new building here, which fits in well. Certainly the new building is cleaner than the old ones and stands out for that reason. But compare the proportion of windows to wall in the new building versus the old ones. The new building is built with modern techniques and modern materials and is able to be structurally stable with less wall and more window; yet it learns from its neighbors and responds to them. It clearly defines and delineates the sidewalk-level pedestrian space from the floors above; there is a cornice line for the penthouses; the windows are well defined.

Portland, OR

Wales, UK

Plant your building so it looks like a hill

Neighbors often complain (with great justice) that a building has "excessive height, bulk, and scale." Sometimes these words are talismanic: archibabble that coats a gloss of academic respectability on the not-in-my-backyard impulse. But often, they are correct. The real culprit is a zoning code that does not require any transition to smaller neighboring properties. For the builder in a site where the zoning code has erred, try to hide the excessive height, bulk, and scale.

Nobody minds living in the shadow of a hill. A hill can be much bigger than any apartment building ever proposed, but no one comments on its size. So plant your building so it resembles a hill. Stepping down a building helps it more closely resemble a natural form.

Seattle, WA

Use a similar roofline

Fitting in the old and the new can be as simple as copying rooflines.

There are few uses whose activities are less compatible with a quiet residential street, yet whose presence is more critical to its safety, than a fire station.

This station was originally built in the 1950s. Fire-fighting rigs have grown longer and taller since then. The firefighters needed to remodel their station to accommodate the newer gear. It would have been very easy for an expanded fire station to be totally incompatible. But the designer linked the remodeled station to its single-family neighbors by size, setback from the sidewalk, and roofline. The roof of the old station was popped up and a new facade added.

The surface treatment of the fire station looks somewhat industrial and differs from its neighbors. But the consistent scale, roofline, and setback allow it to fit in and to be a visual asset to the neighbors.

Vancouver, BC, Canada

Mimic the older building's details

The parking garage on the left side of the photo is from the late 1980s. It works because it mimics its charming older neighbor to the right. The window openings are of the same proportion and line up with each other across the two buildings. The facades appear to be of the same material; the striation of the stonework in the older building is repeated in the new one, as is the cornice line. The garage also has openings at street level to match the older building.

The new parking garage does not "read"— as architects say — as a parking garage but simply as a kindred addition to an older building. You could pass by and not recognize it as a garage.

From the inside as well it is a delight, as the big windows nicely frame the buildings across the street.

Use similar materials

These elegant townhouses sold unfinished for $600,000 to $800,000 in the late 1980s. To one side they are bordered by even more imposing houses and to the other by far more modest structures. But on all sides, brick was common. The new townhouses' brick facades linked them with their neighbors.

Seattle, WA

Look smaller from the sidewalk

People have a thing about large buildings: they don't like them. Whether their feelings reflect groupthink or not, it's a political reality that when it comes to fitting in new structures with existing single-family neighborhoods, small is good.

This supermarket appears significantly smaller than its more than thirty thousand square feet would suggest, because much of its mass is set below the street grade. Where it fronts the sidewalk it is only one story

Portland, OR

high. Furthermore, because it comes right to the sidewalk, it has a traditional and reassuring air.

SMALLER SCALE AT THE SIDEWALK

Seattle, WA

Camouflage the parking garage

This site is within a block of a deep saltwater bay. It is built on fill, and because of the high water table, it was not feasible to allow parking underground. (There would have been a constant battle with seepage into the garage due to the hydro-static pressure on the foundation.)

Thus, the parking had to be placed above grade. Rather than give up valu-able retail space at sidewalk level, the parking garage was placed above the first floor. By bringing down the window pattern from the offices above, the architect created the appearance of a unified whole. One can be aware of this building for years before realizing that its first few stories above the street contain a parking garage.

Paris, France

Make rules but allow them to be broken

A central premise of this book is that a comfortable city's environment is by no means random, subjective, and chaotic, but is composed of many recurring patterns that are, with few exceptions, preferred by all people.

Nonetheless, a healthy city will provide room for new and unexpected design, particularly in visual appearance. All buildings need not mimic exactly their neighbors so long as in some significant way they are complementary. Harmony can be made with dissonant chords. Novelty and surprise are the spice of the city. Let there be exceptions to the rule. A variety of sites, circumstances, and tastes dictate differences and preclude a detailed rule book of cities for all times. Though there are timeless patterns and designs that work, leave room for experiments, especially with someone else's money.

The big proviso is that the builders and public officials must clearly understand what rules are being broken, and why, and have sufficient skill to carry it off. That's a big if, but not impossible. Allow room in the zoning codes to let people try.

North Vancouver, BC, Canada

Celebrate the banal

Gas stations (or electric-vehicle recharge stations) will be with us for some time.
Let even the very mundane be pleasing.

I pulled over to take this picture.

My companion asked, "What's that?"

"A gas station."

"Really?" he replied.

We so expect the ordinary to be ugly that it is a surprise when it is not.

Boston, MA

Sometimes the issue is a minimum rather than a maximum

We are so used to urban battles over the size of buildings that it is refreshing to see a circumstance when the issue is that a building is too small.

For example, some "New Urbanist" codes have build-to lines, which define the *maximum* distance a house can be from the sidewalk, and it is often a rather small distance. The typical suburban code, conversely, will have a *minimum* setback from the front property line, often fairly great.

In this picture, we see a code flaw that seems to have allowed a structure too *small*, rather than too *big*. Amidst three- and four-story structures we see one a third as high. Such a variation breaks the feel of the street. It is an oversight in the code that expresses perfectly the idea that just as we lose weight bite by bite, we build streetscapes lot by lot, and every building contributes to or detracts from its street.

CHAPTER 10

SMOOTHING EDGES: BUFFERS AND SHIELDS

Sharp edges shock. To paraphrase Lord Acton: "Change shocks. Dramatic change shocks dramatically." Sharp transitions in the built landscape are no exception. Nature abhors a sharp transition or a rough edge. The forces of gravity, and of wind and water, tend over any period of time to smooth out sudden, jarring geological boundaries, to create gradual transitions. We avoid rough edges in social conduct, too, with gracious talk and diplomacy. And we do the same with our built landscape.

We build walls for privacy from other people's curiosity. We grow hedges to shield us from the view of the junkyard. We build roofs to keep us dry and houses with operable windows or air-conditioning to keep the heat away. We create buffers so that we can tune in some things and tune out others.

Robert Frost may have spoken ironically: "Good fences make good neighbors." But indeed the defined boundary is an aid to neighborliness, if only because we know where responsibilities end and begin.

City zoning codes create boundaries to separate incompatible functions. Of course, by carrying this separation to extremes, we create the need for cars for even the simplest trips, and hence once again need buffers. For example, consider the typical convenience store. When it is adjacent to residences on its backside — and where else would it be? — the parking lot needs buffering to be a good neighbor. But the buffering is needed not because of the retail use per se but because of its accessory parking lot.

In cities we need buffers from blank walls and also from automobiles — whether in motion or parked. It is particularly our precious cars that we seek to keep at bay. The car is our central nonhuman relationship and urban-design challenge. The purpose of urban buffers is to smooth the edge between the place of cars and the places of people.

What an irony. How perverse. Our most valued places are often sites that exclude our most valued possession: cars. We have roadless areas in the wilderness; we seek to build pedestrian-friendly areas to which we can drive and then walk around. No one is immune. Our own car is a gem, and the freedom it grants is a pleasure. But we love to be in a place without being bothered by other people's cars.

Many of our buffers are ways to avoid the blank wall and visual monotony. Buildings with large-scale users, such as telephone company offices, often meet the street with a blank wall. Security is an issue, but in any case their transition to the street is not considered important by their single-minded institutional owners.

Blankness seems to be an innate human horror. Shelley speaks of Ozymandias's stare as "blank and pitiless as the sun." One common human nightmare is to be chased by faceless beings. Turning one's face away from another is a put-down.

Lewis Mumford explains his generation's rapid adoption of the barren modern style as an overreaction to his parents' generation's horror of the blank wall and their consequent fascination with things. In his autobiography *Sketches from Life,* he says, "The clutter of interior decoration in middle-class homes at this period is almost indescribable. The most contemptuous word that could be applied to an interior in those days was 'bare'— 'as bare as a barn.' I still remember that in one of Conan Doyle's early novels the young heroine was almost driven to insanity when her cruel calculating guardian confined her to a bare, whitewashed room. The bareness did it!"

We decorate to buffer ourselves from blankness . . . from madness.

North Vancouver, BC, Canada

Soften walls

One very common edge is presented by the retaining wall, which is a necessity when lots are small and there are slopes. Some way must be found to create a transition between two elevations.

Often it is concrete, blank, and forbidding. In certain situations it can be softened. The one above is made of interlocking pieces of precast concrete with soil placed in between. Plants grow there, and water can flow through to relieve pressure buildup behind the wall.

Seattle, WA

Screen the parking lot with display cases

Few things are less comfortable than the blank wall. They are boring to walk by and make no contribution to safety: no human surveillance. But sometimes they are unavoidable.

These display cases were allowed by building officials as a substitute for retail spaces. Though a weak echo for the intent of the zoning code — visual interest, security through eyes on the street, and so on — they do effectively screen the parking garage from the sidewalk. They give passersby something to look at and advertise the activities of the museum served by the parking lot.

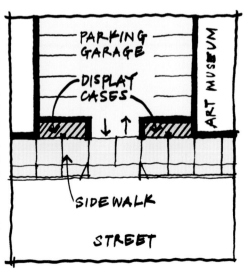

Seattle, WA

Hedge in the entrance

In residential areas, too, the relationship of the house to the sidewalk is important.

Walking on the sidewalk before the gaping maw of a two-car garage and attendant curb cut is not a pleasant or urbane experience, particularly when there are several double garages in a row. In cities with few alleys it is a common experience. There is no other way for a car to enter the site except across the front sidewalk and front yard.

This house solves the problem by narrowing the entry with a hedge, paving the forecourt with bricks and softening the roof edge with wisteria.

In a neighborhood with few muggers this is a very civilized solution. It probably violates the zoning code requirements for sight triangles (how much you can see) at driveways, but it works.

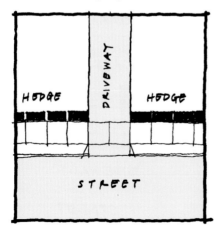

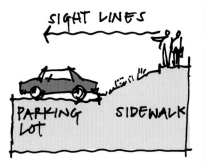

Shield with elevation

Many military tactics use earth forms to take advantage of the enemy. One takes the high ground above the enemy to defend, and one slips through the depressed swale to outflank. Shielding the car from view is similar to defending against any adversary.

This parking lot was set lower than the level of an adjacent sidewalk; one looks over and past the cars. The other lot is set above an adjacent road so that one cannot even see the cars. (So well hidden is the parking lot that when I first reviewed this photo, I could not remember what it was supposed to show.)

Seattle, WA

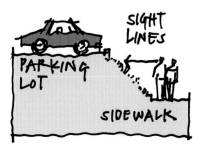

Redmond, WA

Plant street trees for premium value

Even streets of modest houses gain grandeur and presence when treed. Old money need not have a monopoly on old trees.

If time is money, then these street trees are very expensive. Yet a four-inch caliper tree can be planted for merely $300, including maintenance for the first five years, when it is most vulnerable. The expensive part is time: foresight and patience. Cities would do well to spend less energy on contentious greenbelt regulation and more on planting trees on their existing "barrens"— their rights-of-way.

Enjoy the economies of scale by letting landscape contractors bid block by block: not a tree here and a tree there, but blocks, indeed neighborhoods, of varying trees. The homeowner could choose to have a tree set in her curbside planting strip by checking a box on the utility bill, with payments stretched out over some reasonable time.

On an economic basis, street-tree planting will more than pay for itself in increased property values, particularly when done on a neighborhood-wide basis. One tree in front of one house is fine, but the real impact is felt when an entire district is treed.

Planting 150,000 trees on the public right-of-way of a medium-size city might cost each homeowner $60 a year for five years. But the trees would likely boost the value of each home by at least $1,000 to $5,000 at the end of that five-year period. That's a fair return.

Longview, WA

St. Helena, CA

Narrow the parking lot entrance

Neck down the entrance to create a landscaped area. It is an easy way to civilize a parking lot where it meets the sidewalk. This one is a little the worse for wear, but imagine the desolation if these trees were gone.

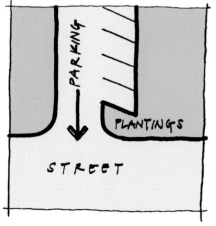

Again, it is these small and modest improvements to the city's physical shape, repeated over and over again, that give a city its vitality and interest and comfort.

Unfortunately, these small items of civic courtesy do not show up in the glossy architectural and design magazines, but they are in fact the truly important items.

Seattle, WA
photo by Barbara Gray

Maintain the parking lot landscape

It takes no high aesthetic sensibility to critique the strip mall. But as nasty as those auto-oriented suburban strips may be, they will be with us for a while. So imagine them with really lush landscaping. Most lots are large enough to accommodate quite a few shrubs and trees, and landscaping is fairly inexpensive. Such a small gesture and so much impact.

Imagine if most parking lots were surrounded by green. We would still have auto-oriented strip-malled neighborhoods. But what an improvement. So let's pass a law, we think. But the key is ongoing maintenance, which is practically beyond the reach of regulation.

Many cities have rules that require landscaping in new construction; some require irrigation systems or the planting of drought-tolerant species. Others even require some nebulous language about continued maintenance. But the key to pleasant landscaping is in the hands of the property owner. What turns the key is the shared social expectation — not the hammer of the law — that taking care of one's property is the decent thing to do. We see this most clearly in single-family neighborhoods, where subtle but real social sanctions are brought to bear on homeowners who let their lawns go unmowed. Such social expectations also command respect in commercial districts and will motivate the property owner to go beyond merely purchasing plants to actually maintaining them.

The larger lesson of this landscaped parking lot is to do small things to make life more comfortable now.

Sidney, BC, Canada

Build green walls when needed

As noted before, not all single-use zoning is unwise. There are indeed unpleasant spillover effects from intense use, even when it is the parking lot of a beautiful garden. This impressive hedge protects neighboring properties from a large and busy parking lot.

Nantucket, MA

Soften with green

Money, that is. The transition from house to car is important, common, and most often harsh. Soften it with decorative paving, which admittedly is very costly. But the choice for a builder of all but the most modest houses is where to put the discretionary money. For a charming place, better cobbles on the ground than tiles on the roof. Patterned concrete — not much more expensive than asphalt — can also work wonders.

Build a grassy berm

We have an approach/avoidance relationship with parking lots. We need them for our personal convenience, but we prefer to hide them.

This berm separates the parking lot from the sidewalk.

Seattle, WA

Make fences low enough to see over

This bamboo fence creates a boundary for the realm of the automobile. Before its installation, in life's inexorable and harsh struggle to park as close as possible to their destination, drivers used to park their cars across the sidewalk. This fence stops such parking and returns the sidewalk to the person on foot. It is low and open enough that it doesn't create a security problem.

Seattle, WA

Trellis blank walls

Blank walls have no personality. They are devoid of human attention. But sometimes they are inevitable. There are ways to make them less offensive, which in this case is by obscuring them with a trellis.

Los Angeles, CA

Olympia, WA

Raise property values with walls

One of the most annoying elements of city life is noise — other people's, that is. In fact, the difference between sound and noise is that you make sound, other people make noise. This is nothing new. Noise has long been the bane of urban life. The diarist Samuel Pepys spoke of seventeenth-century London's unpleasant noise. A very effective torture that leaves no visible scars is to subject a person to enormous and continuing noise.

There are three ways to deal with noise:

- Change its nature at the source. For example, tire producers and road designers could make low noise one of their design goals. Active noise cancellation could actually produce counter-noise to wipe out the objectionable noise.
- Mask it with a more pleasant sound of your choosing.
- Block it with a solid physical structure.

The edge of the freeway is one of the most inhospitable places in the world. Its incessant and insatiable roar is an overall blight. This roar hinders conversation, is bad for mental health, and dampens real property values. The freeway spreads its oppressive, dull, and ever-present Niagara roar far away from Lake Ontario, to every city on the grid.

One way to lessen the roar is with this freeway wall. It is an expensive piece of concrete. But its cost will be easily recaptured from increased taxes because the neighborhoods beyond the wall will become quieter, more pleasant places to live and hence more valuable.

Vancouver, BC, Canada

Use glass to block noise

This wall blocks noise from a very busy arterial and yet permits a sense of the world beyond to the residents behind it.

Use white noise from a waterfall

The white noise of this waterfall masks street noise and makes a park usable.

Seattle, WA

photo by Barbara Gray

CHAPTER 11

WASTE NOT, WANT NOT:
OLD SHOES ARE MORE COMFORTABLE

Old shoes are more comfortable. And safer, too. As the mountaineer Lou Whittaker tells people about to ascend Mount Rainier, "Comfort is safety." Western society, wealthy beyond the dreams of an earlier era, turns to recycling, historic preservation and restoration, adaptive reuse, and discovered spaces. Why? Simple expediency: economics and ecological common sense. But if you listen carefully to people talking about these practices, there is also an undercurrent of discomfort with a rapidly changing world.

Old things reused are a gyroscope to help us keep our mental balance.

How does celebrating, using, and reusing the old make us more comfortable? The short answer is the term "old shoe." What could be more comfortable than the old shoe, so long as it was from the start well designed, sturdily built, and well maintained through its usage. When updated carefully — through new soles or modern plumbing, let's say — old things are fully functional and have the comfort of age. Such old things provide continuity with the past and comfort us.

Our world is changing remarkably quickly and without historic precedent. In no other time in the history of our species has change been so wide and deep and rapid. We see and will continue to see great adjustment in social customs, in the global environment, in local geography, and possibly even in our genes. There have been revolutions of consciousness and matter in the last two hundred years. Even when beneficial, such change can be disquieting and socially destabilizing. Each day we rush forward into a brave new world; the tension increases. Will the center hold? In the past, the man-on-horseback swept into view to provide guidance for a population confused and disenchanted by a torrent of change. The man-on-horseback may yet again ride forth.

People under stress are bait for the tyrant. If we cherish free institutions, then we want a society where people feel at ease and comfortable. Hence it is politically practical and wise for us to incorporate that which we value about the past into our future.

Old things lend stability and equilibrium; old things reused are sound from the simple point of economics. But more importantly, old things reused are a gyroscope to help us keep our mental balance. Old things act as a flywheel. Their familiarity and comfort provide inertia and help us keep our sense of ourselves in a world that seems to reel so rapidly as to spin us off into chaos.

Seattle, WA

Use side yards for seating

The natural operation of human ingenuity draws out all sorts of underused resources. With enlightened planning, or out of a quest for personal gain, the odd, unusual, or awkward space — once thought useless — can be brought to life and made fruitful.

This side yard had been used for automobile parking, but it was on the sunny south side of the building and so was a natural for outside seating. Note the flakes on the lower portion of the wall where it was cut to create access to the cafe through the courtyard.

It need not take a large quantity of room to create a pleasant space. In fact, the intimacy of the space is part of its charm.

Consider the alley (as a retail street)

This alley is more than a service way. It is a thoroughfare with life of its own. When market demand is sufficient, allow shops and businesses of all kinds to front on an alley and create a more permeable surface at a very human scale.

Denver, CO
photo by a Denver friend

Allow alley houses (for economy and safety)

The housing market is varied, and there is demand for dwellings of many sizes. One way to increase the housing stock (and hence put a damper on prices) is to allow "in-law" apartments: small secondary dwellings on the same lot as a house.

Neighborhood opposition intrudes. For most people the purchase of a single-family home is a genuine achievement and major investment. They fear that renters in the neighborhood will mean a lowering of its quality. Part of the solution is design that respects single-family scale.

But increased safety is a benefit of alley houses. Police do not like alleys because the natural surveillance necessary for safety is missing. Houses rarely orient to alleys and there is no constant presence to keep an eye on things. But small dwellings add eyes to the alley.

Seattle, WA

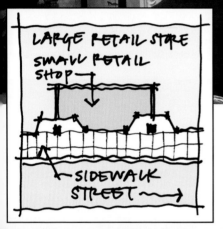

Seattle, WA

Small retail spaces work well

This espresso stand is only six feet deep and about thirty feet wide. It replaced a display window — you can still see the bays — and is an extraordinary example of the power of tiny changes to activate a street.

The land-use code required separating the parking garage from the sidewalk. The ordinary response would have been a blank wall, adding nothing and subtracting much, but the code wisely offered the option of a small storefront. This tiny retail space was the response.

Use roofs for play

Using the roof for activity creates problems for the designer and roofer, but, considering the price of urban land, it may be a worthwhile investment.

Seattle, WA
photo by Barbara Gray

Seattle, WA

Reclaim the International Style plaza

Unfortunately we still follow the well-meaning but misguided fashion of the International Style. Our codes offer extra building allowance to the developer who creates a plaza in front of an office tower. Granted, some recent plazas were well designed from the start, but the world is full of empty, windswept plazas (orphans of the 1950s and '60s) waiting to be filled up with uses that might create a richer and more humane environment.

The good news is that private and public interests flow together here. Filling up those barren plazas can recreate a streetscape for the walker and increase economic value for the building owner. Witness the new retail spaces at the right of the picture. They are a welcome 1980s addition to a 1965 building. One can quibble that the building owners should have gone further and filled in more of the plaza to create a continuous street edge, but this is a good start.

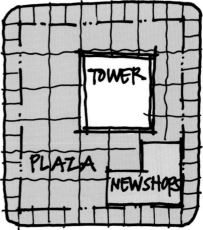

Seattle, WA
photo by Barbara Gray

Bridge freeways to relink neighborhoods

We used to think that we lived in a "cowboy economy" in which we had unlimited resources. Land was considered cheap. With enormous suburban farms waiting for houses, urban land had little special value. The great adjustment of the last thirty years is that we now see ourselves on a planet of great but finite resources. We recognize that we have, as economist Kenneth Boulding phrased it, a "spaceship economy" in which there is no such thing as garbage but only raw materials for reuse.

The airspace above freeways is an enormous pool of undiscovered space, though due to the layers of government involved, tapping it is complex. As urban society implodes upon itself, these air rights over freeways are recognized as a valuable resource.

When Interstate 5 tore through Seattle in the 1960s, the construction was done with little regard to neighborhood impact. It became a noxious canyon, dividing what were once coherent neighborhoods. This convention center and adjoining park were built over the freeway in an attempt to knit back the central business district with an adjoining residential neighborhood.

Bath, England
photo by FreeFoto.com

Place shops on bridges

This bridge shows mixed-use from an earlier era, with a twist.

The story of Pulteney Bridge should be familiar, for it shows how land development and transportation improvements work together. It is the eighteenth century. A landowner wishes to develop an estate across a river from the city of Bath, England, even at that time a major resort. The first and critical step is to build a bridge to provide access to the land. Inspired by the Ponte Vecchio in Florence, shops are built on it to add a bit of Continental glamour and encourage people to approach and cross.

The logic and efficiency of putting shops at a crossroads of that type is impeccable.

Of course, no one could claim that putting shops on bridges is a necessity for a comfortable city. Pulteney Bridge is a whimsical example of discovered space. How could it have any relevance to the modern, auto-oriented world?

Remarkably, "discovering" the space over a divider is actually quite relevant today. A most striking effort to knit together a city torn asunder by an interstate highway is under way in Columbus, Ohio. Named the "I-670 Cap," it is a complex undertaking, requiring coordination among many levels of government, and an imaginative and plucky developer. The Ohio Department of Transportation had originally proposed widening the interstate, requiring a new bridge. In order to lessen the impact of that widening on surrounding neighborhoods, some genius

Columbus, OH
photo by Melaca Architecture

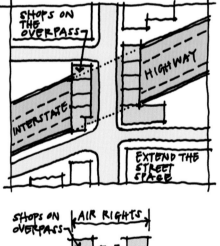

suggested widening the bridge itself to allow 26,000 square feet of shops along with on-street parking. The purpose, as with Seattle's Freeway Park (see page 182), is to create a seamless pedestrian path from one neighborhood to another over the dividing chasm of a freeway. If it is successful, pedestrians will be able to cross the interstate hardly knowing that it is there, aware only that they are walking down a pedestrian-oriented street. Based on the photo above, showing the project under construction in August, 2003, judge for yourself. I think it's a winner.

I believe that this undertaking, while relatively small, is extraordinary and worthy of emulation. It provides a model, reaching far beyond Columbus to the many thousands of freeway overpasses across America, of how to create a seamless transition.

Seattle, WA

Turn leftovers into parks

Street ends are "leftovers," places where the public right-of-way runs into an impassable barrier, such as a lake or steep hill. But these street ends, particularly when on the water, are ideal for little parks.

Why are there street ends at all? As recently as 1900, boats were often the quickest and most reliable way to get around. Earlier society expected to enlarge the street grid by filling the shallows at the water's edge to create more usable land. More shoreline access was an economic advantage. But as economic patterns changed, rather than using the shoreline for commerce people discovered that street ends make excellent parks. Because such efforts are small, they are ideal for neighborhood action. The very first such street-end parks on this lake were built by neighborhood volunteers.

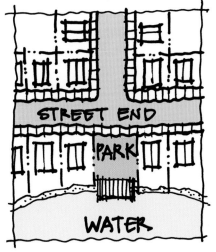

Boulder, CO

Use storm drainage channels for bike trails

Vast areas of the American West are beset by arid conditions with occasional torrential downpours. Such storms can flood surrounding neighborhoods. Many such cities handle storm-water overflows through hardscaping all-year creeks to increase their water-carrying capacity. The single-use drainage system through which Arnold Schwarzenegger rode his motorcycle in *Terminator 2* is a typical desolate example of how it's often done.

Boulder, Colorado, built a system of watercourses to deal with the same problem. But it recognized while designing the project that at most times of the year these riparian corridors are usable by bikers and walkers. The system was designed to accommodate them.

Boulder, CO

Seattle WA

Bring dead corners to life

Corners of a parking garage are generally unusable for parking. The most efficient layout for stalls — ninety degrees, head in — generally leaves a parking space that cannot be used (at least not according to the building code).

But this space is ideal for small shops such as espresso, flowers, and pizza. Such retail spaces at each corner of this garage give life to the street and interest to the building.

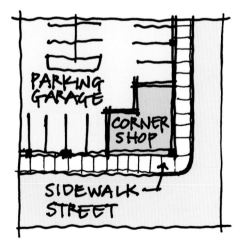

Seattle, WA

Use the air well as a garden

For apartment dwellers or office workers the parking garage may be more important to the way they experience a building than the formal, pedestrian entry on
the sidewalk. Their daily to and fro begins and ends where they park the car.
They may rarely see the lobby.

Yet we give little attention to parking garage design except for narrow technical issues of automobile maneuvering such as aisle widths, turning radii, and
ventilation.

Building codes often require some sort of continuous fresh air in underground

parking garages. Here, the builder created air wells, cutouts in the land as
it runs up against the building. They
were cheaper than mechanical ventilation by fans, and more pleasant.
It created an opportunity to make
parking one's car just a little more
civil by bringing light and air to the
lowest level.

In addition, security is enhanced
because calls for help might be heard
on the sidewalk and in the apartments
above.

Portland, OR

Save even one tree

We so love efficiency that it is surprising when we see a walkway or a road rerouted to save a tree. The trees shown here were poorly located in the first place. They had overgrown their place, were buckling the sidewalk, were out of scale or in the way.

But someone cared and molded the right-of-way around them.

The benefits are several and varied:

- A fine old tree is saved.
- Traffic must slow to negotiate the obstruction.
- People are reminded by its eccentricity that the city need not be managed as a machine for some supposed "efficiency."

The lone tree is particularly striking and a reminder that steering wheels are designed for avoiding obstacles.

Carmel, CA

Los Angeles, CA

Los Angeles, CA

Build around the tree

This newsstand is noteworthy as an illustration of urban backfill. The building owner used some of its private property — an otherwise barren setback — to create a street-enlivening retail site.

But there were some handsome trees in the space. In most situations one would expect them to be cut down. But imaginatively, they were incorporated into the newsstand.

Seattle WA

Use front yards for urban backfill

Even along a very viable retail street there may be properties that are not ready for redevelopment. There may be a variety of reasons, from the inclinations and capabilities of the owner to the size of the property in relation to the zoning. Perhaps, in the latter case, when the zoning capacity is high and the property is small, the logical thing to do is to assemble several small properties into one larger one.

But as an interim until a site is ready for redevelopment — and interim uses can go on for many years — encourage development in the front yard to enliven the street.

Seattle WA

after

before

King County, WA
photos by Peggy Gaynor

Daylight the buried creek

"Daylighting" — as in being reborn — is the process of reviving degraded watercourses by uncovering them. This creek had been buried in a pipe until the designers of a new park saw the opportunity to resurrect it. The transformation is remarkable.

The environmental movement has matured in the last thirty years. It now recognizes that the preservation of a particular landscape or one endangered species is insufficient. The challenge is to save entire ecosystems. And such preservation is moving beyond mere stopgap salvation to restoration.

Nigel Calder's *Eden Was No Garden* describes a future society whose entire culture focuses on restoring degraded lands to wilderness. The political will for such widespread restoration was to be based on our ancient heritage as hunters. In our own day, hunting and fishing enthusiasts could be allies for greens even though blood sports have little place in current environmentalism. It is an intriguing political calculus.

Habitat restoration in cities may seem a barren field. But possibilities exist, particularly with streams. Under every city are many streams that once ran free. For centuries, surface drainage was viewed as much a nuisance as a blessing. Streams were often routed to run underground in culverts, or if left on the surface, used as nothing but a drainage ditch.

San Francisco, CA

Washington, DC

WHISTLER RESORT RECYCLES
• ANY MATERIALS LEFT ON THE
  GROUND DO NOT GET RECYCLED.
• PLEASE DEPOSIT MATERIALS FOR
  RECYCLING INSIDE THE APPROPRIATE
  BIN.
• THE SUCCESS OF THIS PROGRAM IS
  IN JEOPARDY DUE TO MATERIALS
  BEING LEFT OUTSIDE OF THE
  BINS.

Whistler, BC, Canada

Seattle, WA

Make recycling second nature

The hardest step of recycling is the first one: separating items of different categories just before they become garbage. Recycling at home and work has become common. These devices start to make the recycling habit second nature in public, too.

There's no reason why items such as museum guides and theater programs cannot be reused. Even such mundane recycling gets people thinking about where things go.

CHAPTER 12

PERSONALIZING THE CITY WITH ART: "KILROY WAS HERE"

I was riffling through my photographs to organize them for the first edition of this book. I was trying to sort them out into logical categories. Most fell into place quite easily. But I ended up with a substantial pile of photos that did not fall into any particular category of city comforts. These pictures — of murals, sculptures, embedded objects, and the like — were all intended to be (and were generally perceived to be) art.

However, my intention had never been to include art in this book. Of course the objects had appealed to me; I had photographed them. But I had never seen art as an integral part of the land-use issues that were my major interest.

Then I realized that public art is an entirely different animal from art in a magnate's living room, and that public art, too, is about making closer contact.

The world is a big and sometimes lonely place. We are all Robinson Crusoe, going to and fro in search of another comforting human voice, any sign that another person passed this way before, such as Crusoe's found footstep in the sand: the first sign of another human he had seen in twenty-six years.

With art and decoration we personalize our built environment beyond what we need for bare function.

Public art and decoration are a city comfort because they remind us that we are not entirely alone. We see the touch of a human hand, which is comforting in a world of great and faceless natural forces and enormous and anonymous institutions.

> We are all Robinson Crusoe, going to and fro in search of another comforting human voice.

Public decoration is not a comfort because it is art. Whether any particular work is indeed art is beside the point. Argue, if you like, about whether it is art when the work is in private. The important part of public art in public spaces is its larger message: some person, some individual, has passed this way before and has put some of his or her life, time, and attention into making what we see before us. Public art contributes to the process of place making.

Some person has individualized the place and made it less anonymous. The city comfort of public art helps to tune out the void of aloneness.

Public art is a high-class form of graffiti, or at least can stem from the same impulse. It is a marker and statement: "I was here." It is somewhat like the running visual joke of soldiers from World War II, "Kilroy was here," which said nothing but had great meaning.

Take caution. Art, too, can be inappropriate to its location or audience. It can be a threat, like much of the spray-painted graffiti of adolescents, which reminds us of the hostile marking of territory by animals and repels us rather than attracts.

Public art contributes to the process of place making.

Public art functions in one more way: as a conversation piece to foster the casual human exchange that is at the heart of the city's purpose. A piece of public art, or an artist's skilled transformation of some otherwise mundane street furniture, gives us something to observe, ponder, and mention. And there is no more surefire way to start a discussion or to animate one than to ask, "And what do you think of _____?" (Fill in the name of the most controversial public art in your city.)

Approaching public art as a conversation piece may sound like the absolute height of barbarism, at first. However, this perspective does not at all diminish art but heightens its importance. There can be nothing less barbaric than an object that breaks down the barriers between people and leads them into interesting talk.

North Vancouver, BC, Canada
"Totem Pole Project," by Mark George

Have artists work in public

Let public art be created in public so that the work of the artist is not so mysterious. It is not just imagination but motor skills that we admire in them. Furthermore, watching an artist at work is an excuse for people to gather.

Sometimes even gild the lily

It might seem excessive that a bench in a setting so marvelous should itself need decoration. But why not?

Los Angeles, CA

Seattle, WA
Concept and design by Anne W. Knight

Decorate the street's surface

There is hardly a public surface not available and crying out for decoration.

This hatch cover provides access to underground utilities and is also a map of downtown Seattle with a stainless steel button indicating YOU ARE HERE.

The larger social question prompted by these covers is how to create an economy in which it need not take certified specialists (artists, in this case) to enrich the visual environment. How can we avoid a dreary sameness in the elements of our streets by including decoration even in mass production?

Embed things

Engaging decoration can be smooth and unobtrusive.

Seattle, WA

Decorate blank walls with murals

Of course there shouldn't be very many blank walls in cities in the first place. That's one of the basic principles of urban-village design. Blank walls lead to dead streets with no pedestrians, and no people lead to danger . . . and boredom. There are very few blank walls that do not appear to cry out for some covering.

Seattle, WA

Here an old warehouse was built to the common property line. In such cases it is normal to have a very blank and very fireproof wall. But if the adjoining lot is a parking lot, the blank wall is not hidden. What better to do than commission a mural for it?

Art can be temporary

This enormous — twenty feet high —inflatable face was a striking contribution to a Fourth of July celebration. It was up and down in no more than forty-eight hours.

Seattle, WA

Seattle, WA
"Fremont Troll" by Steve Badanes, Will Martin, Donna Walter, and Ross Whitehead

Let art raise a smile

In human activity, the squishier the standards, the more ruthless the competition and the more serious the aura required to convince people to take the whole endeavor, well, seriously. The art enterprise proves this point well. But it places art on a serious, ill-serving pedestal that hinders art's great contribution to comfortable cities.

This troll is out of the way, under a bridge, of course. I drive by it often and have rarely seen it lacking visitors. Perhaps because the troll is so popular, some members of the arts community look askance at it. But they miss the point. It is public art. Therefore the way one judges it must be entirely different than for private work displayed in a private place.

Seattle, WA

"Dancer's Series: Steps" by Jack Mackie with Makers and Chuck Greening; photo by Jack Mackie

Teach dance steps

"Is that the mambo?"

"Yes."

"Are you sure? You couldn't possibly remember it yourself."

"Well, thank you, I guess, but I think you do it this way, then move the left foot that way. Right?"

"Right?"

"No. Maybe it is left. Yes, I think so. Isn't that what it shows? Here's step one, then two . . ."

The natural thing to do with dance steps embedded in the sidewalk is to try them out. Certainly these dance steps are art. But far more important, these dance steps are a maypole around which strangers can weave a conversation.

Seattle, WA
Artwork by Marco Lucioni

Art can clarify

The door to a shop was tucked into an alcove and all but invisible. Many customers went to the store next door by mistake. The solution was to paint an image of a door — a *trompe l'oeil*, a trick of the eye — on the wall adjacent to the real door to point the customer in the right direction.

Bainbridge Island, WA

Refer to art

Port Madison is at a backroads corner on a rural island quickly becoming suburban. Like most suburbs, it has many newcomers. The island is large and it is easy to get lost. But this fragment of glaciation — Frog Rock — gives a reference point, as in "Go to Frog Rock and then turn left."

Seattle, WA

Art can protect us

This sidewalk is directly adjacent to a high-voltage power station. The electrical utility wanted a way to secure the site and keep out vandals. Instead of the standard barbed-wire chain-link fence, the utility's project manager saw the potential. He proposed an artwork to top the existing concrete wall that would shield the station and yet engage pedestrians. The artist responded to this clear program with a fiercely protective yet entrancing "garden" of galvanized flowers.

Seattle, WA
"McGilvra's Farm" by R. Byer

Let children confuse art and toys

Art should not be apart from life on an altar in a museum as if done by gods, but part of daily routine, experienced every day. The artist's imagination can be a good baby-sitter. Build it sturdy and safe so children can play with it.

Seattle, WA

Seattle, WA

Decorate spaces under bridges

The space under a freeway (or bridge of any type, even over water) is usually unpleasant, a derelict wasteland or place of danger through which people try to hurry (trolls lurk under bridges). Take extra pains with such spaces. Lavish care on them so that they reconnect neighborhoods rather than sever them, as they almost always do, by making it more pleasant to walk along them.

The red and yellow columns were painted to connect old and new Asian business districts under an interstate. At another underpass, artists are at work.

Seattle, WA
"Jackson Street Colonnade" by Fire Cruxent

Seattle, WA

Sing in tunnels

Tunnels are grim and uncomfortable, particularly pedestrian ones, reminding people of bunkers and a state of siege. Not surprising: their purpose is to give the street surface to the car so auto traffic can flow unimpeded. Tunnels force people underground and diminish the pedestrian place. Avoid building them. But, alas, some tunnels are inevitable, so at least do a decent job of it.

This one ("The Tunnel Garden," by Richard Posner with Robert Schneider and Ginny Ruffner, Thomas Gerard, Michael Lord, and Syntonics, Inc.) underneath a major arterial connects a university medical center and an underground parking garage. It is decorated in a style somehow reminiscent of some South Seas paradise. Walking through the tunnel, one suddenly hears the sound of chirping birds from an electronic cage. The surprising delight brings a smile and a wonder. What type of bird? Where does it nest? When does it sleep?

Olympia, WA
"Long Instant" by Michael Fajans

Fit art to the place

A classic view of art is that it should explain and exalt the virtues of those who perform extraordinary deeds; it should honor the heroic. Devoting one's life to waiting to enter a burning building to protect strangers must surely qualify.

Olympia's Art in Public Places program commissioned this work for the lobby of a fire station. The painter spent time with firefighters to gain insight into their work. This work speaks more about place than about the artist.

There is sufficient ambiguity, uncertainty, and confusion in the world for us to be able (with little loss) to forgo having the artist insist on sharing it with us. Public art should expand consciousness, not further confound.

CHAPTER 13

WHAT TO DO?

The creation of a comfortable city, or neighborhood, or urban village is ultimately a social process — drawing on the actions of many individuals within a web of social constraints. Indeed, city building is a political process, and increasingly so. Various forces encourage metropolitan areas to grow, with a concomitant growth of environmental regulation.

It's a truism that people get the government they deserve. Similarly, people get the kind of neighborhood they discuss. Intelligent conversation precedes effective political action. Further, it is my belief that it is the individual's understanding and perception that undergirds all collective action.

Feel, observe, analyze

The very first step is to examine the city in your daily to and fro and to pay particular attention to your own reactions, to what you like and what you avoid. People do not perceive the environment in "plan view," as lines on a map, but as a series of details that unfold before them as they move about the world.

Examine your own feelings about different environments and your own preferences. To what places are you drawn? What do you avoid? Then try to analyze what specific things attract and repel you. In particular, pay attention to parking lots and their relation to your destination. A good exercise as you drive around (presumably you do drive around) is to figure out the way in which the building and the street are joined. Imagine yourself in an airplane and look down on your streetscape and see how it is organized.

Tours

Take a daily tour. Vary your route to work each day. An old real estate man once told me of this technique. If done consistently, and with attention, it eventually reveals a great deal about wherever you live.

The physical world is incredibly rich and complex, and many things will pass us by without an expert guide. Investigate your environment in the company of people who work with it on a daily basis, such as architects, planners, and real estate brokers. Each profession will have a different perspective, but one based on its own intimate contact with the material.

Try an organized tour. Check with your local American Institute of Architects, for example. Many local chapters organize walks through interesting areas. While many tours focus on individual buildings, the manner in which these individual urban threads weave themselves together into a diverting whole is more and more often brought to the fore.

Real estate salespeople can provide a wealth of insight, too. Impose on a shrewd real estate agent to show you around; they have a practical and ground-level sense of how your city is organized.

Boat tours are particularly interesting. They reveal how things work from the marine side, now no longer as important as it once was, but of great historic significance. When I visit a city with a waterfront I usually take the harbor tour.

Listen

Another approach is to listen to the language in which we all talk about the environment. What do people observe and find worthy of comment?

One of the subthreads in this book is the importance of the landscape conversation: how we discuss our surroundings, the words we use, our manner of discourse. Since buildings grow out of our perceptions and conversation, a very good place to start thinking about comfortable cities is to listen to your family, friends, and acquaintances. Consider how they talk about the built environment and how that influences their choice of environments.

I believe you will find that the discussion rarely reaches actual things or feelings but is more about abstractions and theories: Will rail work? Are developers greedy?

Friends' day-to-day speech; public speech by politicians, activists, and journalists; and the complex and confused conversation between government and governed in the bulky land-use codes all reveal a great deal about our image of the landscape.

Read

Other people's observations of the world are also extremely important. But they should supplement, not replace, your own direct experience. A great deal of writing on architecture, for example, focuses on the visual appearance of buildings as isolated objects. That is worse than useless to the task of creating comfortable cities, for it misdirects attention to irrelevant matters, to "eye candy." It ignores the behavior of buildings and the subsequent behavior of people. It elevates intellectual abstraction above practical assessment.

These are some of the books that have been helpful to me.

The Death and Life of Great American Cities by Jane Jacobs. The all-time classic proposed that cities are more about messy vitality than neat boredom.

A Pattern Language by Christopher Alexander, Sara Ishikawa, and Murray Silverstein. There are rules and patterns that work, and this book shows what one design group thinks they are. A fascinating book to surf.

City by William Whyte. An examination of public spaces in terms of how people actually behave.

Life Between Buildings by Jan Gehl. A riveting architectural study of the design of public spaces that gets into a lot of (essential) numerical detail.

The Great Good Place by Ray Oldenburg. The first place is home. The second is work. The third place is the social meeting place — the tavern, the coffeehouse, etc. — and is the "great good place" of this book.

Place Makers: Public Art That Tells You Where You Are by Ronald Lee Fleming and Renata von Tscharner. Places grow out of locations. Public art has a large role in such evolution.

Defensible Space: Crime Prevention Through Urban Design by Oscar Newman. The basis of safety is natural surveillance and a sense of territoriality that leads people to take action.

Residential Street Design and Traffic Control by Wolfgang Homburger et al. An authoritative review of methods of traffic calming. Academic in style, but a must-read.

Parking Spaces: A Design, Implementation, and Use Manual for Architects, Planners, and Engineers by Mark C. Childs. A wonderful book that recognizes the central role of parking lots in our culture and broadens, with marvelous specifics, our imagination of what they can be.

Let people spend their own money: revive the LID process

The "Local Improvement District" (LID) is a political framework by which property owners in an area can join together to tax themselves to build improvements — roads, sidewalks, sewers, dikes, what have you — in the public right-of-way or on public property. A significant portion of the urban infrastructure that we have inherited from earlier generations was built through the LID. Two essentials are a clearly defined "benefit area" and a clearly defined monetary benefit for the properties that bear the tax.

Many of the small details shown in this book that improve quality of life are in the street right-of-way. Such improvement shows up in a real increase in property values. There is no reason that property owners should not willingly, even enthusiastically, invest in the public environment adjacent to their properties. After all, the cost of most of these minor details pales into insignificance when compared to the value of the land and its building.

Unfortunately, at least in some areas, property owners are effectively discouraged from making such direct investment in their own neighborhood. Municipal engineering departments are often still auto-oriented and have a culture of discouraging pedestrian-oriented improvements. Making matters worse, some local governments promote a distinct infantilism of their citizenry by discouraging the LID process, preferring to offer back "grants" of their own tax money, money that citizen property owners could rationally increase dramatically if they would only come together through an LID.

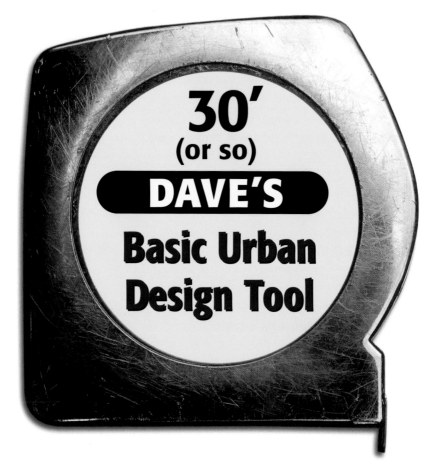

30′
(or so)
DAVE'S
Basic Urban
Design Tool

Carry a carpenter's tape

Taking the Three Rules very seriously, urban design comes down to a matter of feet. A carpenter's tape (with only some hyperbole) encompasses that critical urban design realm.

- Thirty feet or so *out* from the property line into the street right-of-way.
- Thirty feet or so *in* from the property line onto private property.
- Thirty feet or so *up* from the property line to about the third story.

So carry a tape with you — a real one — and measure spaces where you feel comfortable so you can become familiar with what works. Bear in mind that much of our science started with mere observation and measurement. Though there is much talk about scale, it is wise to hone one's sense of it in real numbers.

Urban Cabin™ Condominiums

ON CAPITOL HILL

a True Tale

DAVE: You know, Don, our buyers will like our new urban cabins because these condominiums will be distinguished by their superb dynamic spatial continuity as well as by a component massing that proposes a four-dimensional interplay of those precise yet amorphous elements that are essential to the creation of an appropriate urban contextualism in the late twentieth century.

DON: Oh, for God's sake, Dave! Cut the B.S. and just tell 'em that they're good-looking, well built, and cheap.

ARCHI-BABBLE

Use small words to discuss the landscape

Our buildings respond to our conversations about the urban landscape — from zoning codes to breakfast chat. A comfortable city needs a populace that cares about the built environment, knows what it wants, and has the vocabulary.

But archi-babble — like kudzu — has a way of creeping in and taking over any real conversation about the built environment by channeling conversation into a display of fancy concepts rather than individual feelings. We defeat our own goal of comfortable cities when we use words that confuse the citizens, who should be able and confident to speak with feeling, perception, and precision about the landscape around them. Of course, some technical terms are useful shorthand, but such compression can also act like jargon, and like any jargon can limit important conversation to a self-selecting elite. The city is a social work, and all must take part.

To promote widespread discussion of the city landscape, use small words.

Choose an appropriate standard of review

Our expectations for buildings — old or new — should be modest and realistic. Such realism starts with the perspective — the standard of review — that we use to evaluate them.

We are too harsh with our architects and builders. We somehow expect each new work to be novel and full of surprises. This point of view does not help to create amiable cities. It looks at the wrong things. People — architects included — often speak of a building and decry it as derivative or nothing special. When questioned further, they will readily admit that the building isn't bad, really, but it's not a "great" work.

To wonder if a particular building is a great work is to hold it up to a flawed standard of review on two counts.

First, such an approach tends to overemphasize the purely visual; one examines the building as if it were a photograph on a wall, and one talks of balance and composition and so on.

Second, the very nature of the question asks one to view the building as a discrete object — isolated on its own parcel — not as a piece of a city landscape. The building becomes a piece of urban sculpture, a "precious object."

Both aspects play into the misuse — albeit ancient — of architecture as a tool of social aggrandizement, posturing, and pomposity. Such an attitude may feed the hungry maw of the architecture and design press, but it does little to nourish the eye or body of the would-be urban villager.

This great-work standard is usually grandiose and beyond human scale. Something more modest is needed.

More often than not, the important question is not whether some particular building is a great building. The correct standard of review is more this: If this building were just about the standard for the community, would we still want to live here? Does the building follow the very few basic rules of urban design? If so, grant the permit and build it.

Every town needs a few memorable structures of civic pride and joy: a stadium, a tower, a church or temple. But these are by practical necessity few; the majority of buildings will be (we hope) good, solid, money-making background structures. It is only occasionally that a building — by special use or unique site — needs to be a focal point. Our cities have a long way to go before it's appropriate to apply the great-work standard of architectural review to everything that's constructed.

Let's redefine our standard of greatness so that striving and self-promotion are excluded.

Children should read the plan of their city

The shaping of cities is very much a political process and a product of overall social awareness. It serves future political conversation well to inculcate such awareness early, certainly in the K–12 educational system.

I was reading a biography of Mayor Richard J. Daley and was riveted by one passage:

Burnham's Plan of Chicago of 1909 was greeted with enormous enthusiasm. A popularized version of the plan became a bestseller, and in textbook form it became required reading for eighth-graders across the city. Like most Chicagoans of his era, Daley read the book as a student. This compendium of bold ideas for refashioning Chicago was, he once said, his favorite book.

WACKER'S MANUAL
OF THE
PLAN OF CHICAGO

Municipal Economy

OAKTON COMMUNITY COLLEGE
DES PLAINES CAMPUS
1600 EAST GOLF ROAD
DES PLAINES, IL 60016

Especially Prepared for Study in the Schools of Chicago
Auspices of the
CHICAGO PLAN COMMISSION
BY
WALTER D. MOODY
Managing Director, Chicago Plan Commission

1913

That a city plan could be widely read by children struck me as extraordinary but, on reflection, extremely sensible, for it raises consciousness and can teach the vocabulary required for intelligent discussion. Each chapter of Mr. Wacker's *Manual* ends with questions ranging from the very general ("Name three things created by the movement of mankind to congregate in cities") to the very specific ("How much is the roadway to be raised at Ohio and Lake Streets?").

The idea that a contemporary planning document could be read as a text, in the current sense of that word, as a stand-alone document with meaning, would be remarkable to anyone familiar with the output of our planning agencies. Furthermore, as children are notoriously uninhibited in asking questions, the knowledge that planning documents would be exposed to wide reading — and by children — might have a salutary effect on its drafting.

Applaud good work with precision

The most basic phrase of good manners is "Thank you." The most effective way to receive an encore or repeat performance is to shower the actor with applause. Positive reinforcement is the basis of behavior modification. As a society, we do that far too rarely and with little aplomb. Of course we applaud with money, that is, by buying someone's product. It would help to add this basic tool of good management — thanks and recognition — to the governmental land-use arsenal.

Behind those real estate signs and partnerships there are people. In fact, the real estate development business is singularly entrepreneurial; many sizable operations are the domain of a very few individuals. Like everyone else, they are motivated by more than just money. When developers do good work, show them that we citizens care, and explain very specifically what they have done right in an urban-design sense.

With real estate developers, as with pets and children, it is important to reward good behavior immediately. Otherwise, being unconnected in time, the reward will not relate to a specific action. The reward must be timely and specific, and must explain precisely why the project or element is successful.

Do simple things now

There is a rule of science known as Occam's razor, attributed to a fourteenth-century monk, William of Occam. The rule's essence is that when there are alternative explanations for a phenomenon, we should choose the explanation that has the fewest and least complex assumptions.

There should be a corollary for city planning. We should choose the simplest and most economical means of solving a problem rather than the most complex and expensive. This book is devoted to the idea that we seldom do so. Particularly now that we have established remarkable systems of transport, power, and communications, it is time to consolidate our gains and attend to fine-tuning these systems.

Many athletic trainers believe that the origin of high performance is in simple things such as good breathing. Similarly, the majority of golf professionals will tell you that the origin of a graceful, efficient, and comfortable swing is in the two things you do before you even start the swing itself: how you grip the club and how you stand when facing the ball.

Why do we constantly seek the more difficult path? Rather than facing and tackling the reality of the car and taming it, we argue about and then build expensive systems, either rail or road. The question is more for students of group psychology and organizational dynamics than urban planning and architecture. The answer lies more in personal ambition than in common sense or public interest.

Fighting against the trends though it may be, do simple things now.

Seattle, WA

SOME FINAL THOUGHTS
A final challenge

Some years ago I was returning with a good friend from a tour of the East Coast. We had seen the lovely pastoral landscape and estates of western Massachusetts and Connecticut. We had experienced the elegance (and grit) of New York City, and the splendors of the Metropolitan Museum of Art and its gift shop.

And then we landed in Seattle. The sky was typically gray. It was a letdown to be back. I started complaining about how shabby the city looked and how Seattle's built environment in no way measures up to the brilliance of its natural setting.

My friend agreed and then, in her absolutely sincere and comically perverse way, turned and said, "Which leaves us a tremendous opportunity to improve things. It's not as though we live in Paris — what would we do then?"

Olympia, WA

Sleeping in public

Lying down in public and dozing in the sun can only be done in a safe place. Perhaps the city has never been a place where one could let down one's guard, even though the city started as a place of refuge from the dangers — natural and human — of the wilds.

But this is an appropriate scene upon which to end this book, and a hope for the future. One person who read this book in its earliest stage questioned me, "Why put a picture of the homeless in a book devoted to comfortable things?" I was taken aback; I had no idea what she meant until she showed me the man lying on the lawn.

I had photographed this man asleep because he presented what I thought to be a pretty picture and a worthy goal: a city of such security and ease that a well-dressed businessman (as I saw him) would feel comfortable taking an after-lunch nap lying on the lawn of a park. My reader friend saw a homeless man asleep during the day, when, ironically but understandably, it is safer for the homeless to sleep.

That is the goal: to build a city so comfortable that one may lie down to rest, safely, in public.

THE END OF THIS BOOK

But hardly the end of the work.

There is much more to be said about how to make our cities comfortable, and even much more to be done.

Human beings are endlessly ingenious in making the environment more comfortable. The world is enormously rich with designs that work. One of the difficulties (and delights) of finishing this book has been the enormous richness of the built environment. It seemed as if there was another good idea around every corner that needed to be tracked down. An idea's absence from this book means only that we ran out of pages or didn't know about it. We can provide more pages. You can help fill in the gaps.

The world is enormously rich with *designs that work*.

We continuously search for specific examples of designs, patterns, prototypes, and ways of doing that work to make city life more comfortable. Simple things are welcome. In fact, the more mundane and ordinary, probably the more often used and therefore the better.

One final point: if you think that the majority of details shown here are essentially ordinary and banal, you are absolutely correct, and that is the whole point of this book. Applying imagination and consideration to the ordinary and banal produces a comfortable and gracious place to live.

Please suggest other comforts for future editions. If you have better examples or images of comforts already shown in this edition, we'd welcome them as well. We will give you a copy of the new edition if we use your idea or image.

City Comforts Inc.
david@citycomforts.com

INDEX

Comments on the first edition

"I was in the office of a prominent Vancouver landscape architect firm, responsible for some of the most important new projects in the city, and there on a desk was a copy of *City Comforts*. Not surprising, really. Except this copy was absolutely jammed with stickers and notes, almost doubling the thickness of that little volume. Clearly, *City Comforts* was a miniature encyclopedia for these urban designers.

"So my advice to potential purchasers: buy two. *City Comforts* is the kind of book easily worn out from overuse."
— Gordon Price, Councillor, City of Vancouver, BC, Canada

City Comforts (1st ed.) at work with landscape architect Don Wuori of Phillips Wuori Long Inc., Vancouver, BC, Canada

"Clear, to the point and constructive."
— Jane Jacobs, *author of The Death and Life of Great American Cities*

"*City Comforts* is terrific. It is a wonderful delivery system."
— Andres M. Duany, Town Planner

"I had *City Comforts* in my hands for only ten minutes when I found something we could use."
— Grant Natland, Calgary Parking Authority

"*City Comforts* reminds us that there are literally hundreds of little things — both functional and beautiful — that make a successful urban place."
— Peter Katz, *The New Urbanism*

"After you've read your copy of *City Comforts*, send it to your city supervisors."
— J. Baldwin, *Whole Earth Review*

About the Author

David Sucher lives in Seattle, Washington. He likes to ski, sail, play golf and observe cities.